D0361891

Salvadorans in Suburbia

THE NEW IMMIGRANTS SERIES

Allyn & Bacon

Series Editor, Nancy Foner, State University of New York at Purchase

Salvadorans in Suburbia:
Symbiosis and Conflict

Sarah J. Mahler
University of Vermont

Allyn and Bacon
Boston • London • Toronto • Sydney • Tokyo • Singapore

For Salvadorans everywhere
past, present and, especially, future

Copyright © 1995 by Allyn and Bacon
A Division of Simon and Schuster
160 Gould Street
Needham Heights, Massachusetts 02194

All rights reserved. No part of the material protected by
this copyright notice may be reproduced or utilized in any
form or by any means, electronic or mechanical, including
photocopying, recording, or by any information storage
and retrieval system, without written permission from
the copyright owner.

ISBN: 0-205-16737-3

Printed in the United States of America

10 9 8 7 6 5 4 3 2 1   99 98 97 96 95

Contents

Foreword to the Series

The United States is now experiencing the largest wave of immigration in the country's history. The 1990s, it is predicted, will see more new immigrants enter the United States than in any decade in American history. New immigrants from Asia, Latin America, and the Caribbean are changing the American ethnic landscape.

Until recently, immigration was associated in the minds of many Americans with the massive influx of southern and eastern Europeans at the turn of the century. Since the late 1960s, America has again become a country of large-scale immigration, this time attracting newcomers from developing societies of the world. The number of foreign-born is at an all-time high: nearly 20 million foreign-born persons were counted in the 1990 census. Although immigrants are a smaller share of the nation's population than they were earlier in the century—8 percent in 1990 compared to about 15 percent in 1910—recent immigrants are having an especially dramatic impact because their geographic concentration is greater today. About half of all immigrants entering the United States during the 1980s moved to eight urban areas: Los Angeles, New York, Miami, Anaheim, Chicago, Washington, D.C., Houston, and San Francisco. America's major urban centers are, increasingly, immigrant cities with new ethnic mixes.

Who are the new immigrants? What are their lives like here? How are they redefining themselves and their cultures? And how are they contributing to a new and changing America? The *New Immigrants Series* provides a set of case studies that explores these themes among a variety of groups. Each book in the series is written by a recognized expert who has done extensive in-depth ethnographic research on one of the immigrant groups. The groups represent a broad range of today's arrivals, coming from a variety of countries and cultures. The studies cover a wide geographical range as well, based on research done in different parts of the country, from New York to California.

Most of the books in the series are written by anthropologists. All draw on qualitative research that shows what it means to be an immigrant in America today. As part of each study, individual immigrants tell their stories, which will help give a sense of the experiences and problems of the newcomers. Through the case studies, a dynamic picture emerges of the way immigrants are carving out new lives for themselves at the same time as they are creating a new and more diverse America.

The ethnographic case study, long the anthropologist's trademark, provides a depth often lacking in research on immigrants in the United States. Many anthropologists, moreover, like a number of authors in the *New Immigrants Series*, have done research in the sending society as well as in the United States. Having field experience at both ends of the migration chain makes anthropologists particularly sensitive to the role of transnational ties that link immigrants to their home societies. With first-hand experience of immigrants in their home culture, anthropologists are also well positioned to appreciate continuities as well as changes in the immigrant setting.

As the United States faces a growing backlash against immigration, and many Americans express ambivalence and sometimes hostility toward the latest arrivals, it becomes more important than ever to learn about the new immigrants and to hear their voices. The case studies in the *New Immigrants Series* will help readers understand the cultures and lives of the newest Americans and bring out the complex ways the newcomers are coming to terms with and creatively adapting to life in a new land.

NANCY FONER
Series Editor

Acknowledgments

There are many, many people I wish to acknowledge, people whose assistance has been critical to this book in a multitude of ways. To those who I inadvertently leave out, I beg your forgiveness *de ante mano.*

First and foremost, I wish to thank the Salvadorans whose voices appear in this text and the many more who I spoke to and whose voices, hopefully, are well represented here. They confided in me defying cultural and legal barriers and many have become lasting friends and confidantes. I was also welcomed warmly by their family and friends in their home towns in El Salvador, a reception that has had an abiding and endearing impact on me. Special thanks to Cristóbal Rosa and Tránsito García who appear in this text incognito but who I wish to publicly recognize as saviors of my reputation during times of great need. Thank you from the bottom of my heart.

Next I wish to give my appreciation to my colleagues and friends at CARECEN: Oscar Salvatierra, Alizabeth Newman, Patrick Young, Ken Lederer, Arnoldo Lemus and many others. They have had an enormous contribution to the lives of thousands of Salvadorans on Long Island. Sue Calvin deserves special recognition. Not only does she work at CARECEN, but she doubles as a wonderful photographer. Credits for the cover photo go to her. There are several other organizations who serve Salvadorans as well who deserve mention and appreciation. Centro Salvadoreño, The Workplace Project, CEPA Mujer, La Fuerza Unida, La Unión Hispánica, and Catholic Charities, in particular.

I would also like to thank several leaders in the Salvadoran and Latino community who provided information to me during my research. They include Omar Henríquez, Pat Blanco, Helen Bonilla, Cecilia Morán, Nubia López, Esperanza Quesada, Luis Hernández and Emilio Ruíz.

There are many institutions and friends within them who I wish to acknowledge as well. This book was written in large part while I was a visiting scholar at the Russell Sage Foundation in New York. I thank everyone at RSF, particularly Eric Wanner, for making my home there so comfortable and collegial. My fellow visiting scholars provided endless stimilation, especially my colleagues engaged in research on immigration: Alex Stepick, Min Zhou, Victor Nee and Nancy Foner. Thanks to Nancy also for her excellent work as editor of this book series. Much of the research for this book was conducted through grants from the John D. and Catherine T. MacArthur Foundation and the University of Pittsburgh's Center for Latin American Studies. Last, but not least, many thanks to my colleagues at the University of Vermont who have supported me over the past three years. The Anthropology Department has provided a wonderful home and a great academic foundation. Thanks to my colleagues: Robert Gordon, William Haviland, Carroll Lewin, Kenneth Marty, William Mitchell, Marjorie Power, Steven Pastner, and Peter Woolfson. Special thanks to Carol Anne Wheel and Michael Crowley (my research assistant) for their expert help in preparing the final manuscript.

Several colleagues not already mentioned above have been of great help and support during the past years. They include Saskia Sassen, Alejandro Portes, Max Castro, Katherine S. Newman, Marcelo Suárez-Orozco, Roger Rouse, Judith Martí, Christian Zlolniski, Victor García, Salvador Cortés, Michael P. Smith, Tommie Sue Montgomery, Deborah Anker, Clara Rodriguez, Josh DeWind, Harrison White, Michael Schwartz, Edward Funkhouser, Reynolds Farley, Herbert Gans, Peter Guarnaccia, Carol Stepick, Leah Haus, Kari Winter, Eugenia Georges, Steven Rubenstein, Jean Scandlyn, and

Claire Cesareo. Thanks also to Sylvia Shepard, my editor, for her skillful work in shaping up this manuscript.

Many other people on Long Island and throughout the country also provided important information and friendship during my research. They include Pam Goldberg, Esq., Judy Rabinowitz, Esq., Lolita Fonnegra, Rev. Bruce Page, Sister Fancis Gritte, Robert Warren and Michael Hoefer at INS, Elizabeth Comitino, Steve Valli, Lynn Gomez, Frank Medina, Helen Hopps, Mark Stamey and Bruno Bembi, Esq.

Finally, my family merits perhaps the greatest recognition. To my husband, Boanerges, and daughters, Sophia and Priscila, thanks for letting me be absent, albeit only temporarily. Thoughts of you always make the work go faster and the end shine brightly, giving me the strength to continue.

Introduction

The Latino population in the United States has been growing rapidly over the past decades and early in the twenty-first century Latinos are expected to become the largest minority in the country. They have already achieved this status in several major cities including Los Angeles, Miami, San Antonio and New York. In 1960 the U.S. census recorded 6.9 million persons of Hispanic descent or 3.9 percent of the total population; by 1990 this figure had jumped to 22.4 million people or 9 percent of the total population (figures exclude Puerto Rico's population). Fertility rates and immigration are the two principal factors responsible for this rise in the Latino population. Although Latinos share similar historical and religious backgrounds, social structures, customs and the same language largely due to their common roots in former Spanish colonies, they are also very diverse. Many are immigrants but most are native-born; they also vary along national origins, class, racial and ethnic, and residential lines. An appreciation of both the forces that unite and those that divide them is key to analyzing the contemporary role Latinos play in U.S. society and to predict their future role. This book is written as an introduction to one new Latino population which has received little scholarly attention to date: Salvadorans.

The literature on Latinos in the United States is dominated by texts devoted to the study of the three largest subgroups—Mexicans (13.5 million according to the 1990 U.S. census), Puerto Ricans (2.7 million) and Cubans (1 million). Salvadorans form the fourth largest group (565,000), yet little has been written about them, presumably because they arrived much more recently. Few Salvadorans resided in the United States until the outbreak of civil warfare in El Salvador in 1979; during the next decade, hundreds of thousands of Salvadorans fled their embattled homeland and the majority sought refuge in the United States. Tens of thousands settled in New York City and its suburbs, including an estimated 60-100,000 on Long Island. Each Salvadoran has both a personal narrative and one threaded together with thousands of others into a common fabric, into a social memory of the war's human toll.

The purpose of this book is two-fold. First and foremost, my intention is to provide an intimate portrait of Long Island Salvadorans. Their story, told principally in their words, tells about why they left their country, why and how they migrated to the United States, how they have been received by the people and government of the United States, what their daily life is like, and what kinds of changes and challenges they face. Second, this portrait of Long Island Salvadorans reveals a type of migration that has been little recognized and studied—international migration directly into suburban areas. Although suburbia has been home to more of the U.S. population than the cities or the rural areas since 1970—and to increasing numbers of immigrants—immigration continues to be identified with the inner city, the legacy of the Chicago school of sociology. The research I conducted on a suburban immigrant population offers the opportunity to challenge the prevailing stereotype of the suburbs as homogenous havens of the white middle class and it documents that immigrants are becoming an important part of suburban life. Moreover, the Salvadoran migration, while unique in its own way, also reflects much larger social and economic changes occurring in the U.S. at the close of the twentieth century.

SUBURBIA: MODELS OF CREATION

In the twentieth century the United States has been transformed from a rural nation into a suburban society. In 1910, 62 percent of the population resided in the countryside, 26 percent in the central cities and only 12 percent in suburban areas (Wattenberg and Scammon 1972:73). By 1970 and for the first time in U.S. history, the plurality of the population was suburban. Currently, about 50 percent of the U.S. population lives in suburbs while central cities contain some 25 percent each. The suburbs have not only gained people at the expense of the cities, but they have also attracted hundreds of thousands of jobs as well. By 1980, there were almost twice as many manufacturing jobs in the suburbs (11 million) as the cities(6 million) (Baldassare 1986:7).

The earliest usage of the term suburb is from the fourteenth century; from that time through the mid-eighteenth century "suburbe" designated a "'place of inferior, debased, and especially licentious habits of life'" (Fishman 1987:6). That is, in the premodern city the elite were concentrated in the central area and the poorer classes pushed toward the outskirts. This distribution still holds for some contemporary cities such as Paris, Rome, Rio de Janeiro, Cairo and Cape Town, but it is not true for American cities (Jackson 1985). In the United States suburbanization has been more extreme than in other places such as Europe, perhaps due to the greater availability of land. But there are other forces driving this distinct suburbanization and numerous models have been developed to explain the American suburban phenomenon. I will discuss four, the models I label as (1) classic or ecological, (2) aesthetic, (3) economic, and (4) policy or incentive, and then provide a brief discussion of their utility to understanding contemporary immigration to these areas.

The classic or ecological model is attributed to the Chicago school of sociology of the 1920s whose study of urbanism reflects a Social Darwinist perspective. According to this model, competition for space drives spatial organization so that the "strongest" inhabitants of the city occupy the best locations while the "weaker" are relegated to the least desirable areas (see Hannerz 1980). The suburbs are thus an outgrowth, not a simple extension of the city. They were built as places of refuge and exclusivity for the middle and upper classes from the "invasion and succession" of immigrants, the poor and industry into the inner city. Ernest Burgess (1925) illustrated this residential patterning through a diagram of concentric circles, each marked by a set of social characteristics. The inner circle, zone one, is the business district, followed by a "zone in transition" marked by ghettos and immigrant neighborhoods, next a working class area with older immigrant populations, then a middle-class residential zone, and finally a commuter zone.

In contrast to the classic model, the "aesthetic model" of suburbanization views suburbia as a distinct bourgeois invention of eighteenth century London, "the outcome of two opposing forces, an attraction toward the opportunities of the great city and a simultaneous repulsion against urban life" (Fishman:26), that was later adopted by elite and middle-class Americans. According to this vision, suburbia is not just a type of residential patterning, but one which also expresses the values of bourgeois culture.

From its origins, the suburban world of leisure, family life, and union with nature was based on the principle of exclusion. Work was excluded from the family residence; middle-class villas were segregated from working-class housing; the greenery of suburbia stood in contrast to a gray, polluted urban environment. Middle-class women were especially affected by the new suburban dichotomy of work and family life. The new environment supposedly exalted their role in the family, but it also segregated them from the world of power and productivity. This self-segregation soon enveloped all aspects of bourgeois culture. Suburbia, therefore, represents more than the bourgeois utopia, the triumphant assertion of middle-class values. It also reflects the alienation of the middle classes from the urban-industrial world they themselves were creating (ibid.:2).

In sum, the aesthetic model of suburbanization depicts the conscious creation of a physical and social environment that would stand in contrast to both urban and rural settings. Suburbia's aesthetics attracted residents who came for green grass, space, good schools, lower taxes and to escape the racial and ethnic diversity of the cities. "More than anything else, they came because the suburbs symbolized the Good Life....The suburbs symbolized 'making it'. They came by the millions" (Birmingham 1978:vii).

The "economic model" views suburbanization more in terms of economic than aesthetic factors. While the elite built estates in the suburbs for summertime and weekend recreation (e.g., LaGumina 1988), the vast majority of suburbanites were attracted to these outlying areas because of lower costs of living and expanding employment opportunities. Improvements in transportation facilitated both commuting from suburban residential areas to city jobs and the movement of manufacturing and service companies to the suburbs where rents and other costs were less expensive (Stanback 1991). As the suburbs became more populated, they created new demands for retail stores, public services such as schools and hospitals, and consumer services such as child care and cleaning, which, in turn, generated more local jobs. Finally, the newer infrastructure of suburbia became more attractive to businesses as the inner city infrastructure aged (Kasarda 1995). Although suburbia may have been initially constructed as an alternative to urbanity, over time the suburbs became more and more like the cities. As industry and commercial development moved in, suburbs took on the semblance of the metropolis. One author labels this phenomenon the creation of the "technoburb," and claims that with its rise, "the history of suburbia comes to an end" (Fishman 1987:17).

Finally, there is what I refer to as the "policy or incentive" model, which has been argued by historian Kenneth T. Jackson in his book *Crabgrass Frontier* (1985) and by sociologists Douglas S. Massey and Nancy A. Denton in *American Apartheid* (1993). They contend while there are spatial and aesthetic dimensions to the growth of American suburbs, their expansion is much more the outcome of federal government policies that made suburban home ownership feasible for enormous numbers of people in the U.S. As Jackson observes, the metamorphosis of Americans' "penchant for homeownership" (1985:7) into their procurement of titles to suburban homes is mostly the handiwork of the federal government. "The American suburb," he states, "was transformed from an affluent preserve into the normal expectation of the middle class" (ibid.:216). This was achieved largely through government policies that attracted the white working and middle classes into the suburbs. They were offered mortgages on new houses that were cheaper than rents on old apartments in the cities.

The history of these policies stems from the Great Depression of the 1930s when the federal government intervened to protect many homeowners from foreclosure. Trying to prevent massive defaulting on mortgages—which would have deepened the economic crisis—the Home Owners Loan Corporation (HOLC) lent homeowners over $3 billion between 1933 and 1935 to refinance over a million mortgages (ibid.:196). HOLC created a system of appraising real estate before it would approve these loans, a rating system that "undervalued neighborhoods that were dense, mixed, or aging" (ibid.:197). Commonly referred to as "redlining" because poor areas and those occupied by racial minorities were always outlined in red pencil on residential maps, the practice directed most resources toward affluent and suburban neighborhoods and towns populated by whites. At the same time as it founded HOLC, the government created the Federal Housing Administration (FHA) through the National Housing Act of 1934. A major aim of the FHA was to make housing more affordable in order to stimulate the construction industry during the Depression. The FHA began to secure mortgages for up to 90 percent of the home's value; this dropped the typical down payment from 30 percent to just 10 percent of the total price (ibid.: 204).

The federal government's involvement in housing began as a widespread emergency measure but quickly became preferential to certain sectors of the U.S. population. This prejudicial impact intensified after World War II, favoring the suburbs. Under the Servicemen's Readjustment Act of 1944 (the GI Bill), the FHA and the Veterans Administration (VA) were responsible for helping 16 million soldiers and their families purchase homes. Developers bought huge tracts of land and began mass manufacturing housing for veterans, who eagerly snapped up these homes with their government-backed mortgages. Whole swaths of Long Island were transformed from onion and potato fields into suburban towns overnight, the most famous of which is Levittown in Nassau Country. Because FHA financing continued to avoid areas considered risky, the beneficiaries of this mass suburbanization were overwhelmingly white. Another barrier facing racial minorities was residential covenants. For example, blacks were expressly excluded from Levittown by a covenant which stated that "No dwelling shall be used or occupied by members of other than the Caucasian race, but the employment and maintenance of other than Caucasian domestic servants shall be permitted" (*New York Times* June 28, 1992).

Thus, the policy or incentive model argues that at this time whites did not flock to the suburbs in massive numbers to escape an invasion by immigrants and minorities. Nor were picturesque surrounding and the promise of jobs the primary draws. Rather, it was largely government incentives that enticed working and middle class whites to leave the inner cities. The federal government made it cheaper for them to live in suburbia than in the city; at the same time, the government disinvested in cities by contributing few dollars into rehabilitating older housing. These policies fostered urban decay and residential segregation. (Jackson 1985:206)

Suburbia: Homogenous or Heterogeneous?

Despite their differences, all four models of suburbanization imply that suburbs in the United States are viewed as more desirable places of residence than the central cities. The corollary to this, and stated explicitly in some of the models, is that suburbs have been populated overwhelmingly by relatively affluent whites to the exclusion of minorities. Those immigrants and native-born minorities who migrate into suburbia do so as they become middle-class, and are accepted by, "mainstream" American culture. Some new evidence does not fit this pattern. African-Americans, Puerto Ricans, Asian-Americans and other groups have been flocking to the suburbs in the 1980s and 1990s despite continued prejudice and resistance by whites (Fong 1994; Grier and Grier 1988; Rivera-Batiz and Santiago 1994; *Newsday* April 4, 1995; Scandlyn 1993; New York Times May 15, 1994). Moreover, as I observed among Salvadoran immigrants on Long Island, many newcomers migrate directly to the suburbs; they do not become suburbanites after achieving socioeconomic mobility in the city. They come, rather, with backgrounds as peasants and urban workers, and they have limited formal educational training and few skills. Previous generations of immigrants with similar backgrounds flocked into the cities and toiled in manufacturing industries. Why has this not been true for Salvadorans on Long Island? Does the movement of Salvadorans into suburbia reflect changes in the economy, employment availability or other structures of opportunity? If so, can this study of a group of immigrants in a specific region of the U.S. shed light on processes that affect the country overall? These are key questions that I will address in this book.

This study of Salvadorans in suburbia also offers a way to examine pervasive stereotypes about suburbs: their homogeneity, insularity and conformity. These stereotypes seem to be rooted in the mass production of suburbia which followed World War II and were illustrated in a poem written by Malvina Reynolds in 1963:

LITTLE BOXES

Little Boxes on the hillside,
Little Boxes made of ticky tacky,
Little Boxes on the hillside,
Little Boxes all the same.
There's a green one and a pink one
And a blue one and a yellow one
And they're all made out of ticky tacky
And they all look just the same.

And the people in the houses
All went to the university,
Where they were put in boxes
And they came out all the same,
And there's doctors and there's lawyers,
And there's business executives,
And they're all made out of ticky tacky
And they all look just the same.

And they all play on the golf course
And drink their martinis dry,

> And they all have pretty children
> And all the children go to school,
> And the children go to summer camp
> And then to the university,
> Where they are put in boxes
> And they come out all the same.... [1]

In the 1950s, a large body of literature written for the popular market depicted suburbs as socially homogeneous and conformist (Kramer 1972). One of the most influential books of the time was *The Organization Man* in which William H. Whyte argued that the suburbs were the "corporation brought home. They were socially engineered by their residents according to management principles learned at work" (Kramer 1972: xvii). By the 1960s this one-dimensional portrayal was heavily criticized stimulating the publication of works portraying suburbia as more socially diverse (e.g., Berger 1972 [1961]; Gans 1967; Kramer 1972). Still the 1950s "homogenous" image has persisted. Indeed, suburbs contain street after street of single-family homes equidistantly placed alongside curvilinear roads, with fences and driveways demarcating private space, ownership, and independence.

In her 1988 book, *The Moral Order of a Suburb*, M.P. Baumgartner resurrects the notion of suburban homogeneity and links it to a "moral minimalism" defined as the attitude whereby "people prefer the least extreme reactions to offenses and are reluctant to exercise any social control against one another at all" (1988:3). Suburbanites can retreat into the sanctuaries of their homes and cars where they are much more insulated from their neighbors and from street life than their urban counterparts. Thus, if they find something disturbing, Baumgartner argues, they employ the technique of avoidance or they protest secretly to officials who can handle the matter on behalf of the anonymous complainant. But Baumgartner also perceives that the homogeneity of suburbs (presumably she means racial homogeneity) makes it easy for

---

1.   From the song "Little Boxes." Words and music by Malvina Reynolds. Copyright 1962 Schroder Music Co., renewed 1990. Used by permission. All rights reserved.

residents to recognize outsiders even if they do not know their neighbors very well. This leads to some crucial questions. How do suburbanites react when significant numbers of outsiders move into their community? Do they pursue a nonconfrontational strategy or do they suspend their "moral minimalism" for more strong-arm tactics? These are some of the questions I explored while doing fieldwork among Salvadoran immigrants on Long Island. For two years I lived in a town I call Goldcoast (a pseudonym) where I observed an older suburb's reaction to the influx of Salvadorans and other Latin American immigrants.

METHODOLOGICAL AND ETHICAL ISSUES

When I began my original field research on Long Island in the summer of 1989, the vast majority of Salvadoran immigrants there were undocumented. The greatest challenge to me was to locate them, people who lived in the shadows of the law and in the margins of American society, and to gain and hold their trust, their *confianza*. I had to find a way to earn this trust so that they would tell me their stories in their own words, particularly the horrible details of the war in El Salvador. I knew that it would not be easy—that trust is "both an honor and a burden, for it implies a responsibility to help people in a wide variety of ways" (O'Connor 1989:2) and is built over time. I decided that the best way to build this trust and establish entrée with Salvadorans was by offering something of myself, some mutual exchange. I set out at the beginning of my fieldwork to trade my knowledge and services for their knowledge and experience.

The knowledge I had to offer was several years of training and casework experience in immigration law as a bilingual paralegal (counselor). In 1987 and 1988, I had served as a paralegal in immigration law at the Center for Immigrants Rights (CIR) in Manhattan, drawing upon my fluency in Spanish to assist immigrants in political asylum hearings and prepare various applications to send to the Immigration and Naturalization Service (INS). During my fieldwork I also worked closely with several immigrant agencies, most notably the Central American Refugee Center (CARECEN) in

Hempstead, Long Island, where I began a legal clinic on Saturdays providing assistance for immigration-, job- and housing-related problems. I trained several Central Americans to assist clients; the casework we handled enabled me to meet many different immigrants, interview them informally, and help them with their predicaments. This proved to be extremely beneficial for establishing trust as well as a positive reputation within and among people in different immigrant communities.

I also came to serve as a "culture broker," providing rides to immigrants, translating their mail, taking them and their children to appointments, and calling employers to explain absences. My involvement ranged from simple acts such as writing a letter for an illiterate immigrant to send to his family, to sustained interactions similar to a social worker's. For example, I accompanied one woman to her prenatal visits and then assisted her during her daughter's birth. The result was that I became a link in immigrants' networks—perhaps not an indispensable one but at least an important one to many of the people I came to know. As our lives were woven together and as immigrants learned that I could be trusted, they began to tell me things that they did not feel comfortable confiding in others, even close family or friends. Over time, mere acquaintances became key "informants." (Anthropologists use the term "informant" to signify a person who provides information; it should not be confused with "informer" or spy.)

Among many Salvadorans I met, I became a window into a world they could not comprehend very well, the world of the "gringo," the American way of life. Time after time I was the first "American" (a term I use gingerly since Salvadorans are from the Americas too) they had encountered who could speak to them in their native language. This facilitated communication and I was continually peppered with questions about American customs or immigration laws. More rarely, I encountered suspicion and reticence to talk. I anticipated that this would occur, given that I was working with people fearful of detection by U.S. government authorities, and mapped out a three-part methodology that helped me build trust gradually.

During the first six months or so of my fieldwork, I devoted most of my time to researching and exploring the whole island to see where immigrants lived and under what conditions. Long Island (Nassau and Suffolk counties) is over a hundred miles long and home to some three million people. I started by searching for the communities where most Salvadorans settled, but I also wanted to get a sense of the different types of communities they lived in. During this initial stage, I spent a couple of days a week at a safe house, or sanctuary, for undocumented immigrants in Suffolk County. From the 30 or so residents of this small house my contacts snowballed; many of the residents continue to be principal informants although they have long since moved out of the house and pursued their lives in different areas. During these first six months I also gathered contacts through my association with CARECEN and the legal clinic in Hempstead. I visited many English as a Second Language (ESL) classes and church congregations, explaining my research and requesting immigrants to fill out anonymous questionnaires. Finally, at this time I searched for a town which would be a good place to conduct a more community-based fieldwork approach. In February of 1990 I moved into Goldcoast where I lived in an apartment owned by an immigrant landlady who provided housing to many undocumented Salvadorans in the neighborhood. It was only two blocks from a controversial shape-up (a place where day laborers congregate to seek work) which had divided the community. For months I spent the early morning hours with workers as they waited to be picked up for day-labor jobs and as police cars monitored their activities. (In 1995, I was eating breakfast in a small town in El Salvador when a man at the same table told me he recognized me from the shape-up!) The rest of my research time was spent talking to people on the streets, sharing conversations, meals, beers, and information with them, providing legal information and services, and going to their institutions such as churches and parades.

The third phase of my research involved conducting extensive interviews among informants with whom I had developed strong relationships during the early phase of my research. Some of these interviewees were found through the

"snowball" method (Cornelius 1982), when one person intro-
duces the researcher to others. In every case, I waited to ask
permission to interview someone until I had known that person at least six months and we had trust in one another. The
interviews generally lasted five or more hours and often required several reschedulings due to informants' demanding
work schedules. Finally, I supplemented this primary research with data from the 1990 census and information from
secondary sources such as newspaper articles, books, jour-
nals and historical archives.

Information contained in this book is also drawn from follow-up research I conducted in 1994-5. This involved exam-
ining the status of close informants (most of whom I was able
to locate and revisit several times) some five to six years after
originally meeting them. In a few cases, informants had returned home. In 1995 I traveled to El Salvador to visit them
and the communities that have sent significant numbers of
their residents to Long Island. I was able to meet a couple of
informants who had returned, see them and their families in
their own setting. I also met many relatives of Salvadorans on
Long Island who had not returned. I brought with me news
from Long Island, and when I returned to the U.S., I delivered
photographs of immigrants' families and special items which
are difficult to purchase in the U.S. such as cheese and *conser-
vas* (candied fruits). Finally, I have met and observed both in
El Salvador and in the U.S. *viajeros*, personal couriers who
travel back and forth between the two countries carrying
money and other goods. In short, my U.S.-based research has
been supplemented by transnational research which has
added a new dimension to my understanding of Salvadoran
immigrants' lives.

Methodological Limitations

Taken together, the varied methods I have describe comprise
what is commonly referred to as "ethnography," the heart of
which is participant observation. Participant observation involves living among the people researchers are studying and
participating in their day-to-day activities. The strength of
this type of research is that anthropologists learn about the

meanings people attach to their activities and are able to compare what people say they do against what they actually do. Researchers who work with large datasets must take at face value the answers that people have given to their questions, but anthropologists tend to be skeptical of the validity of answers to questionnaires in large-scale surveys since people may well want to cover up the "truth" instead of offering it freely. At the same time, of course, anthropological research has its own dilemmas. To what degree does an anthropologist's account accurately reflect the "reality" of the people being studied or to what extent does it reflect the researcher's subjectivity or the subjectivity of the limited number of informants spoken to? These questions lie at the heart of contemporary anthropological debates and cannot be resolved here. However, the issue of sampling is one I wish to address briefly.

Generations of anthropologists have worked in small-scale communities where it was possible to know everyone and have at least spoken with each individual. In these small-scale communities, anthropologists generally took full censuses of the population; they did not have to base their research upon a sample of the total population in order to document patterns for the larger group. Anthropologists like myself who work in urban settings do not enjoy the luxury of knowing every individual in a population under study. During my 18 months of formal research time (from 1989-1990, and another 18 months afterward when I continued to live in Goldcoast and maintained ties to informants), I could not possibly have located and spoken to each Salvadoran on Long Island. Consequently, I had to work with a sample of this larger population, a sample that could not possibly have been drawn randomly given the nature of undocumented immigration. Without a random sample, I faced the problem of how representative my non-random sample was of the whole Salvadoran population on Long Island. I used several methods to minimize the possibility of selecting a biased sample—a group of Salvadoran informants who did not reflect the diversity of the entire community. First, I located Salvadoran informants through several types of institutions and who lived in different towns. I also included a survey in my methodology and collected over 200 responses. I then used these data, although not collected at random, to compare against the data I collected from the intensive, qualitative interviews with 30 individuals. Another way of verifying information was to interviewed hundreds of other immigrants informally at gatherings such as church events, dances, parties and so on.

All of these sources of data have been integrated into the analysis presented in this book, and together they give me confidence that the stories told on the following pages are in fact representative of the experiences of the broad Salvadoran population on Long Island. Moreover, I took advantage of casual encounters to ask immigrants basic questions about their family, occupation and place of origin. When, after dozens of such conversations I received similar responses, I felt confident that the information provided in a key informant's taped interview was accurate. Through these informal contacts with people, I was also able to doublecheck, understand, or clarify points raised in the taped interviews. Whenever necessary, I also consulted people with longstanding contact in the Salvadoran communities to help me resolve any remaining quandaries. Consequently, the detailed ethnographic evidence offered in this book has been selected to shed light on common experiences and dilemmas Salvadorans have faced. As much as possible, this is done through translated interviews which I hope provide readers with a much richer comprehension of Salvadorans' experiences than could be portrayed through statistics or my second-hand interpretations.

Ethical Concerns

Anthropological research is intense and demanding; it does not end by closing a book and turning out the light. Frequently, I would be called late at night by informants with crises and then find it difficult to sleep. But the greatest challenges came when my credibility was questioned. This happened twice during my fieldwork, once when I was accused of being a spy by some Americans working with Salvadorans and once when I was accused of being a witch by my suspicious landlady in Goldcoast. This type of experience is shared by many anthropologists. Our profession is unusual and we do not fit well into established occupational categories. We spend lots of time hanging around others, talking to them, and then recording the information. This closely matches images of spies, and though we know this, it is little consolation when such accusations jeopardize our fieldwork. Without going into too much detail, let me say that I was able to overcome both accusations primarily because Salvadorans came to my defense against my accusers. I believe that their trust in me was the outcome of careful cultivation on my part, particularly the services and information I provided for them. The case of Roberto Morán (a pseudonym) is illustrative. Shortly after I interviewed Roberto for his political asylum case, I was accused of being a spy and part of the evidence mounted against me was that I had recorded information during his interview. Roberto vehemently defended me which was key to my ability to proceed with my research. He ultimately won his asylum case a year later and I was completely vindicated, but if he had not trusted me in my time of need the pardon would have been meaningless.

Trust is not just critical to fieldwork, it is an essential component of anthropological ethics. There were several other steps I took to foster trust and protect informants' confidentiality. First of all, I explained who I was and what the purpose of my investigation was to Salvadorans I met. This was not always easy since so few had had much formal education and none had ever met an anthropologist before. Second, I asked for their informed consent to be interviewed when I conducted formal interviews. Third, I limited the amount of identifying information contained in my fieldnotes (such as last names and physical descriptions) and I assigned pseudonyms to informants when writing about them such as in this book. This was particularly important since the information I gathered was largely about undocumented immigrants and I could not guarantee that it might not be subpoenaed one day by government officials. Aside from being careful to establish trust with informants before interviewing them, I always conducted interviews in a place where no one else could overhear our conversation. These strategies proved critical to relaxing people so that they would be forthcoming about their experiences during the civil war. Rarely could they speak freely in their residences because their roommates, housemates, or visitors might have served with the military or guerrillas; they were still fearful of being associated with one side or the other for the sake of their families living in El Salvador. I knew individuals so well prior to their interviews, that I recognized when details of stories I had heard before were left out. I then would ask people if they would talk about these details or if they preferred to have the tape recorder shut off to protect their privacy.

ORGANIZATION OF THE BOOK

The rest of this book is organized in the following way. Chapter 1 provides demographic information about Salvadorans in the U.S. and on Long Island and discusses their precarious legal status. Chapter 2 examines the Salvadoran civil war and how it drove hundreds of thousands of people to make the perilous journey across several borders and into the U.S. In chapter 3, there is a detailed analysis of Long Island's economy and how Salvadoran immigrant workers and their established Long Islander employers have reached an economic symbiosis. Chapter 4 depicts everyday life for Salvadorans on Long Island, including the ties that bind them and the forces that divide them. Finally, in chapter 5, there is a discussion of the fact that despite Long Islanders' reliance on Salvadoran labor, Salvadorans have not been welcomed as neighbors in many communities. Indeed, there is growing resistance to their presence. This and other factors do not paint a rosy future for this group of Salvadoran immigrants.

Salvadorans in the U.S.— Status in Limbo

The sun would not rise for another two hours on that fateful day in February 1989 when Juanita Hernández de Argueta roused herself to rekindle the fire in the kitchen area of her home. The children were all sleeping in their hammocks, but her husband, Jesús, was busily packing his few belongings for his trip to United States. Juanita prepared eggs and tortillas for her husband as she always did, but folded many of the thick, warm corn tortillas into a piece of cloth for Jesús to eat on what she knew would be a very long trip. Father then woke each of his children to say good-bye. His eldest was only fifteen and Jesús worried that the government soldiers or the leftist guerrillas would try to recruit him to fight in the civil war, but Jesús needed to leave a man behind to take care of the family and make sure that the crops were planted and harvested. Juanita would be busy raising the five others, particularly the twin girls who were only a year and a half. Jesús kissed them last—the *chamacas* (girls) he called them, not knowing when he would next see them and whether they would remember him at all.

The moon shown brightly as Jesús opened the door of his one-room home and passed into the brisk morning air. He had to leave early, before sunrise, so that his neighbors would not find out he was going until later and to avoid the possibility that the army or the guerrillas would intercept him along the way. No one had been told about his departure except his wife; the children were notified only the night before so that they would not tell their friends. Jesús left home in the middle of El Salvador's civil war when it was risky to trust anyone, even close relatives who he had known all his life. A few months later I met him. He was homeless, unable to pay rent even for a bed. Jesús arrived on Long Island in February, two months before the landscaping seasons would begin and there was no work for him until then. During his unemployment he deepened his debt to his kin; he owed them for the cost of his trip and his expenses in the U .S.—thousands of dollars in all. When at last he received some income, almost every penny was spent immediately to repay his loans and to send money back to his wife. During our first conversations, Jesús never spoke of hardships he faced in the U.S., only those he escaped in El Salvador. Over time, however, he revealed a disillusionment with life in the U.S. and a deep longing to return home. His story is typical of Salvadoran men from the countryside.

This short personal story, like others in this book, are powerful reminders that, although migrations are formed by large groups of people and tend to be patterned, each migrant has an individualized experience. Through ethnography, anthropologists are able to provide an intimate portrait of often impersonal phenomena such as large-scale migrations. We can show how macro-level forces such as conflict and the globalization of industrial production and capital flows impact and impinge upon the lives of everyday people all across the globe. This book is about one such group of people, Salvadoran immigrants to Long Island, New York. In less than a generation, El Salvador has been irrevocably transformed into a culture of migration. Since 1979 when the civil war erupted, an estimated one million Salvadorans—one-sixth of El Salvador's population—have fled their homeland and resettled in the United States. Their imprint can be felt in many communities in the United States and it is indelible in El Salvador itself. Not even the most remote hamlets, like Jesús', have been untouched.

Salvadorans do not travel as far to reach the United States as many other contemporary immigrant groups. Their country lies closer to New York than New York is Los Angeles. But the social distance most Salvadorans travel—the difference between the type of lifestyle they had in their homeland and the life they now lead in the United States—dwarfs the physical distance traveled. Most people in the United States are several generations removed from living on the land. But the majority of the Salvadorans I studied on Long Island journeyed from small village agricultural life to late twentieth century suburbia in days or weeks. This change is abrupt, if not shocking, and there is also little time to make the adjustment. Understandably, their story is not always a happy one. As with any immigrant group, the Salvadorans have had to face many challenges, but, for a variety of reasons, theirs has been a particularly difficult journey.

OVERVIEW OF SALVADORANS IN THE UNITED STATES

According to the 1990 United States census, Salvadorans constitute the fourth largest Latino[1] population, after Mexicans, Puerto Ricans and Cubans. To those who know that El Salvador is a tiny country the size of Massachusetts, this may come as a surprise. El Salvador lies on the Pacific coast of the Central American isthmus, tucked between Guatemala to the north, Honduras to the east, and Nicaragua to the south. In 1979, civil war broke out in El Salvador and continued until 1992 when peace accords were signed between the warring factions. During the intervening years an estimated 70,000 people died, most of them civilians, and hundreds of thousands more fled the country. The war is the direct cause behind the migration of the vast majority of Salvadorans currently living in the U.S. According to statistics maintained by the INS, the rate of legal migration to the United States from El Salvador was very low until the 1980s. In the decade of the

---

1. I prefer to use "Latino" as an ethnic label over "Hispanic" since it links Salvadorans closer to their Latin American heritage over their Hispanic or Spanish heritage. The use of these two terms is a topic of hot debate both among those of Latino heritage and among those who are not Latinos (Oboler 1995).

1930s only 673 Salvadorans migrated and in the 1970s, 34,000 came. By the 1980s, the numbers of legal immigrants had risen to 213,000 (U.S. INS 1991). These statistics offer only a small window on the total Salvadoran migration because most Salvadorans who have entered the U.S. in recent years have done so as undocumented immigrants. The term "undocumented" signifies that these individuals lack the proper papers required to be in the U.S. Many people refer to them as "illegal immigrants" or "illegal aliens"; I prefer the term undocumented because it is less pejorative and because, as I shall explain shortly, Salvadorans have had a long, complicated, and often unjust history of immigration statuses.

Scholars usually cite an estimate of roughly one million for the total Salvadoran population in the U.S. (Montes Mozo & García 1988; Mahler 1995; Funkhouser 1991). This is double the figure enumerated by the 1990 census. I, and my colleagues who research Central American immigrants in the U.S. and who provide services to these populations, are skeptical of the census figures. My disbelief is informed by work I performed for the census itself. I was hired to conduct an alternate enumeration of a Salvadoran community on Long Island. This meant that I surveyed the same neighborhood as the census, counting all the individuals residing there, and comparing my information with that gathered by the census. I found that the vast majority of the Salvadorans living in this neighborhood were not picked up by the census, due primarily to their crowded and unusual housing arrangements (see Mahler 1993). A large number of people I met were illiterate and therefore could not have filled out the census form themselves. They depended on housemates to do this work. This affected the ability of the census to enumerate them correctly because the person filling out the census form might not view newcomers as true members of their household. Particularly in the first year after their arrival, Salvadorans moved frequently in order to take advantage of job opportunities or to find cheaper or more convenient housing. These and other findings lead me to conclude that the census not only undercounted Salvadorans—by at least fifty percent in my fieldsite—but it also disproportionately undercounted Salvadorans with lower educations and job skills. Although I doubt the representativeness of the census data for Salvadorans, it is still the best source of general information available and does help give a broad picture of Salvadorans at the national level and on Long Island.

The half million Salvadorans counted by the census are highly concentrated in only a few states. In 1990, 47 percent lived in the Los Angeles metropolitan area, 11 percent in greater New York, 9 percent in Washington, D.C., 8 percent in San Francisco, and 7 percent in Houston. The convergence of Salvadorans in so few places is not surprising. Like most immigrants, Salvadorans migrate to places where they already have friends or family. This "chain migration," travels along established networks. In more extreme cases, the chain migration is so tight that a town in the U.S. will be populated primarily by people from one town in El Salvador, as in the migration from Intipucá, El Salvador (at the southern tip of La Unión department) to Washington, D.C. (see Montes Mozo & García Vásquez 1988). A similar situation exists on Long Island where people from Polorús (at the northern tip of La Unión department) have settled predominantly in Glen Cove (in northern Nassau County) and those from Concepción de Oriente (also in La Unión department) have gone to New Cassel (in central Nassau Country). Although Salvadorans from each of El Salvador's 14 departments are represented on Long Island, the majority are from only two departments: La Unión and Morazán. These departments are in the easternmost section of El Salvador, an area that experienced the heaviest fighting during the civil war. In contrast to Long Island, Los Angeles has a Salvadoran population that is more representative of all the departments. Despite its size, the Los Angeles Salvadoran community still maintains links to home towns in El Salvador. There are at least a dozen voluntary associations in Los Angeles which unite migrants from the same hometown. These associations hold fundraisers to sponsor projects such as the building of youth centers in their home towns. They are key players in the strengthening of transnational ties. Several home town associations have also been formed on Long Island.

National and Local Demographics

The 1990 census provides a national profile of Salvadorans (see U.S. Department of Commerce 1993). The vast majority are immigrants; only 106,000 of the 565,000 enumerated by the census were born in the U.S. Salvadorans' median age is 25.4 years (about eight years younger than that of the entire U.S.), and the population is split almost equally between males and females. Regarding education, one-fifth of adult Salvadorans (over age 25) have had fewer than five years of schooling, one-third have earned high school diplomas and only about 3.5 percent hold college degrees. Median family income was $22,000 or about $425 per week. In broad comparison to the greater U.S. population, Salvadorans are poorer, younger and less educated. These statistics reflect the fact that most Salvadorans were peasants and urban workers in their homeland, people who were abruptly uprooted by the civil war.

There are an estimated 60,000 to 100,000 Salvadorans on Long Island. This estimate is provided by the leading agency that works with Salvadorans, CARECEN (Central American Refugee Center), a figure which differs significantly from the 19,152 Salvadorans found by the 1990 Census. In addition to the Salvadorans found on Long Island, there are other significant populations in New York City (particularly in Jamaica, Queens) and in other parts of the greater New York metropolitan area. My research has focussed almost exclusively on the Salvadorans living on Long Island, but it is important to note that these populations are mobile and some of my informants have lived elsewhere or have friends and family in other communities outside Long Island.

The data I use to characterize the Long Island Salvadorans in broad demographic terms are derived from the 1990 census and from 202 questionnaires I collected from adult students in English as a Second Language (ESL) classes in several towns during 1989-90. What emerges from these data is that the Long Island Salvadoran migration has been male-dominated (men outnumbered women by at least 15 percent on Long Island in 1990), and that most Salvadorans have low levels of formal education. The 1990 census found that among adult Salvadorans over the age of 25, 18 percent had less than 5 years of formal education, 38 percent were high school graduates and only 16 percent had attended some college. In my survey I found as many as 32 percent had fewer than 5 years of education, 16 percent were high school graduates and only 6 percent had attended college. The census data are probably skewed toward higher educated individuals, people who, as the most literate members of the household, may have been the ones to complete the census form and may have excluded information on some household residents. My guess is that the people I surveyed in ESL classes, who had the time and motivation to learn a new language were also more educated that the overall Salvadoran population.

My apprehensions with these quantitative sources of data are based on my fieldwork and interviews with professionals who work with Salvadorans. Our impression is that the typical Salvadoran on Long Island is from a rural peasant family in eastern El Salvador who has less than five years of schooling. While most of these immigrants are men, I have noticed a rise in the number of women in the last few years. Because migration requires marshalling at least some financial resources, and often large sums of money such as the $2000 Jesús Argueta paid for his trip, it is generally not the poorest people who migrate. But in the Salvadoran case, the war disproportionately affected farmers in the rural areas. Forced to flee, they sold their wordly belongings—the livestock or land—and borrowed money to finance their trips. Consequently, the Salvadoran migration follows more closely a refugee pattern than most migrations.

Salvadoran immigrants earn low wages. According to my survey, they typically earn $900 per month, from which they pay $300 in rent and send $300 home, leaving them only $300 for all of their other needs. Since Long Island is an expensive place to live, this salary level places most Salvadorans among the working poor. Moreover, constrained by a lack of fluency in English, they find it difficult to move up the social ladder. In the 1990 census, seventy percent of Salvadorans in the U.S. over the age of five characterized themselves as speaking "poor" English. People I met were desperate to learn English but constantly bemoaned how difficult it was to learn, particularly given its irregular pronunciation patterns. Children learn quickly however, often pushing their parents to speak English even at home.

Though most Long Island Salvadorans are from the countryside and did not have much opportunity to go to school, there are some highly-educated professionals and business people in the Salvadoran community. Their numbers are rising as the migration matures and more Salvadorans who have grown up on Long Island graduate from high school, attend college, and then pursue careers. Generally speaking, the class character of a migrant population is related to the group's ability to achieve socioeconomic mobility in the United States (e.g. Borjas 1990). The more education and skills (known as "human capital") an immigrant group enjoys, the greater its chances of achieving success in the United States. As compared to other contemporary immigrant groups, the Salvadorans possess a lower level of human capital, more like Mexicans than most Asian groups. Asian immigrants from such countries as China, India, Korea and the Philippines on average have higher educational achievement levels than the overall U.S. population. They migrate to the U.S. seeking better remuneration for their skills than they can achieve in their homelands and many have been quite successful. The future for Salvadorans is much less bright. This is not only due to the fact that they received little formal education back home, but also to their immigration status.

SALVADORANS' IMMIGRATION STATUS

The vast majority of Salvadoran immigrants entered the U.S. without proper authorization. They would have liked to enter legally but this was virtually impossible given the war and immigration laws. Most were too frightened to file the correct paperwork for legal tourist or resident's visas (green cards) at the U.S. embassy. They also knew their applications would be denied. Poor people are routinely denied tourist visas and people without close family living legally in the U.S. have virtually no chance of obtaining a green card. Even in 1995, most Salvadorans have not been able to obtain permanent legal status to reside and work in the United States. As a result, in the eyes of the U.S. government they are "illegal;" in contrast, many advocates of immigrants' rights feel that Salvadorans were unfairly denied their rightful status as refugees. To these advocates, only the treatment of the Salvadorans, not the immigrants, has been illegal.

When people are labeled undocumented (or illegal) immigrants it means that they have done one of two things. Either they entered the United States "without inspection" (EWI) by a U.S. immigration official or they entered with inspection, i.e. with a valid tourist visa or other entry document, and then overstayed the amount of time they were authorized to spend in the U.S. Everyone prefers to enter legally because an undocumented person cannot reside or work lawfully in the country. But most Salvadoran immigrants in the U.S. entered this country without a visa. This is because it is nearly impossible for Salvadorans to obtain a tourist visa from the U.S. embassy in El Salvador unless they are quite wealthy. They must "prove" to the consuls that they are unlikely to stay in the U.S. if they are issued a tourist visa, and to do this they must present documentation of assets held in El Salvador. Normally, this involves showing ownership of a car, a house (and preferably a business as well), the possession of a steady, professional job and a well-endowed, active bank account. Additionally, during the war most Salvadorans were too afraid of reprisals to apply for refugee visas while still in their country. The combination of poverty and fear discouraged almost everyone from contemplating applying. One close informant who was a store owner in El Salvador illustrated the difficulty to me. "If you go to the U.S. embassy to get a visa," Don José Prudencio explained, "you have to have a good job, a bank account, and the title of a house. If you present yourself for a visa at the U.S. embassy with these things, then they will give you a visa so you can travel as a tourist. But if you don't have this, they won't give it to you. It's true too that not everyone will get a visa even if they have all of the prerequisites. Two to three hundred persons go to the U.S. embassy every day and they may give a visa to 20 or 10. Of these 200 people, perhaps 10 percent will get a visa. It's almost a loss to go to the U.S. embassy. So people come *mojado* (as wetbacks)."

Obtaining Permament Legal Status

Even though Salvadorans enter the United States illegally, there are several ways they may obtain temporary or permanent legal status. Salvadorans have pursued every one of these avenues. Permanent residents are most commonly known as "green card" holders. A green card is the colloquial label for the I-551 or permanent resident card. Before the 1980s these cards were actually green, hence their name. Currently, they are red, white and blue with an "INS" hologram on the face of the card and a series of number codes on the reverse. (Their design has been changed to make them more difficult to counterfeit than the old green cards.) Most Salvadoran legal residents were petitioned for by relatives who are either legal immigrants or citizens because the main U.S. immigration law passed by Congress in 1965 emphasizes a policy of family reunification. As the number of applicants rises, so too does the time Salvadorans must wait to receive green cards. Only a couple of years ago, spouses and children of Salvadoran green card holders had to wait only two or three years to emigrate legally. This may seem like a long time, but the period is steadily rising. Currently, they are likely to wait four to five years and the separation can be devastating to families.

The other primary way used to obtain legal status was through a legalization program approved in 1986. In that year Congress overhauled its immigration policy in order to deter illegal immigration. It approved the Immigration Reform and Control Act of 1986 (IRCA) which set up a program to legalize certain categories of undocumented immigrants (those who entered the U.S. prior to 1982 and others who had worked in agriculture). Nation-wide, 150,000 Salvadorans qualified for this program, 8,000 in New York State and 4,000 on Long Island. Later, these new legal permanent residents qualified to petition for their family members under family reunification provisions, a phenomenon that dramatically increased legal migration from El Salvador in the 1990s. Unfortunately, many Salvadorans find themselves in the unpleasant position of having their paperwork in process but waiting years without work authorization for the ordeal to be over. Sonia Acevedo and her children know this anguish all too well. Sonia's husband obtained a green card through the legalization program but Sonia, who immigrated to the U.S. in 1986 to rejoin her husband, arrived too late to qualify. The couple had two more children and the expense of maintaining the family overwhelmed them. Sonia's husband petitioned for her and her elder son who had been born in El Salvador but demanded that she return to El Salvador with the children to wait for her immigration papers to come through. While Sonia waited in El Salvador, her husband entered into a relationship with another woman who bore him several more children. Sonia received almost no assistance from her husband during this time and, desperate, she decided to return to the U.S. illegally to work. One month after she arrived, she received a notice of her residency interview at the embassy in El Salvador. But Sonia got the letter too late. She missed that interview and later applied for another interview that is scheduled for April 1996. Her husband has refused to assist her; she still needs him to file papers showing that he will be financially responsible for her and her son but he will not oblige. Now Sonia does not know if she will ever get her green card.

There is another, less traveled route to obtaining permanent residency. Employers may sponsor their employees for permanent resident status, but this is a long, expensive process. Salvadoran women who work as nannies and have no other alternative to legal status frequently pursue this avenue, despite its long wait and high cost. They must expect to wait at least a six years after paying a lawyer several thousand dollars in fees to receive a green card. A job petition is a much less secure way to obtain residency, partly because it must be proven that the immigrant worker will not displace an American worker. Many of the jobs Salvadorans find require no special skills and it is very difficult to prove that a Salvadoran immigrant is necessary for the job.

With so few pathways to obtain permanent legal status, many Salvadorans wait, hoping that the U.S. government will pass a law that benefits them. They know, however, that in the current anti-immigrant climate their chances of this happening are very slim. Many, wait for a new "amnesty" a new legalization program like the one authorized under IRCA. But IRCA was a double-edged sword. IRCA also legislated employer sanctions imposing fines on employers who hired undocumented immigrants as workers. Prior to this law, it had always been unlawful for undocumented immigrants to find employment; but it had not been illegal for employers to hire them. Now fees are imposed on employers who knowingly hire unauthorized workers.

When employer sanctions went into full effect in 1988, thousands and thousands of undocumented Salvadorans scrambled to obtain work authorization. Many were threatened with termination if they did not obtain these permits or *permisos* in Spanish. Some employers are very strict about checking the documents of their employees and new hires, while others just *echan mirada gorda* which means they look the other way. The INS has not pursued compliance with employer sanctions very forcefully making the risk of fines minimal, especially for small employers like landscapers and restaurant owners. But it has become increasingly difficult for Salvadorans and other immigrants to find work unless they can show work authorization.

Obtaining Temporary Legal Status

Many Salvadorans on Long Island and in the U.S. were able to receive permission to stay temporarily in the U.S. and to work during my fieldwork. In several cases, I assisted them in their application processes. The story about how this opportunity was created after many years of effort is somewhat long and technical. I will provide an abbreviated discussion here (see Mahler 1995 for more details), emphasizing the human impact the process has had on my informants.

Political Asylum

During the 1980s hundreds of thousands of Salvadorans fled the civil war and sought safety in the United States. Many were caught by INS officials upon crossing the border. Some were able to convince the INS that they were Mexican and were deported back across the Mexico border and not to El Salvador. From the border they easily re-entered the U.S. Jesús, for example, faked a Mexican accent when he was caught by *la Migra* (INS). He was returned to Mexico and during his next border crossing he was not captured. Salvadorans who are caught and do not successfully pretend to be Mexican are frequently incarcerated in detention centers until they were brought before a judge at a deportation hearing. If they are lucky, they obtain an attorney who informs them of their right to apply for political asylum. Asylum is very similar to applying for status as a refugee but asylum applicants make their requests from within the U.S.. Refugees apply from outside. Internationally, there is a long history of people seeking asylum or safe haven from persecution, but asylum has had a short history as a legal concept (Silk 1986). In 1967, the United Nations formalized the concept. The U.N.'s Protocol Relating to the Status of Refugees defines a refugee as any person who

> ...owing to a well-founded fear of being persecuted for reasons of race, religion, nationality, membership of a particular social group or political opinion, is outside the country of his nationality and is unable or, owing to such fear, is unwilling to avail himself of the protection of that country.

In 1968, the United States adopted this definition and similar language was used in the 1980 Refugee Act passed by Congress.

The basic concept behind refugee and asylum laws is that people should not be forcibly returned to their countries if they are likely to be persecuted there, the principle of "nonrefoulement." Consequently, if an undocumented person applies for political asylum in the United States during a deportation hearing, the deportation is supposed to be stalled until the claim can be decided. If the claim is not frivolous, if it seems to have some merit, the INS regulations say that the applicant has a right to work authorization while the case is being adjudicated. Applicants for asylum may often, but not always, be able to obtain their release from the detention center by posting bond.

Until the very end of the 1980s, only a trickle of Salvadorans applied for political asylum. They feared that, by filing an application, they would be seen as taking a political stance against their government. They were reluctant to do so because they knew that if they returned home or were deported, they would be targeted for retribution by the government and maybe even killed. Moreover, they feared that their statements might not be used just against them but against their family members still living in El Salvador. I experienced this fear first hand. I counseled hundreds of Salvadorans regarding asylum and it was invariably difficult to convince them to apply because they knew the information would not be kept confidential. Indeed, asylum hearings held in immigration court are open to the public. The other reason few Salvadorans applied for asylum was that it was almost impossible for them to win their cases. During the 1980s only 2.6 percent of Salvadoran applicants were granted asylum. In marked contrast, 62 percent of Iranians applying during this period won their cases, 60 percent of Rumanians, 37 percent of Afghans, 25 percent of Nicaraguans but only 2.1 percent of Guatemalans and 2.0 percent of Haitians. As these patterns repeated themselves year after year, refugee, church and legal organizations began to question the equity of the refugee/asylum process. Many believed that the granting of safe haven was controlled by politics not humanitarianism. As one scholar argues, "support for a government normally implies denial of refugee status to its nationals" (Zolberg et al.1986:155).

Salvadorans avoided applying for political asylum throughout most of the 1980s unless they had been picked up by the INS and placed in deportation proceedings. If this happened they had little choice but to apply for asylum in order to prevent their deportation. But when the Immigration Reform and Control Act of 1986 (IRCA) was passed and employer sanctions went into effect, Salvadorans and other undocumented immigrants became desperate for any means to obtain work authorization. Their desperation was taken advantage of by people who promised to obtain work authorization for them for a fee, usually $350 or more. In reality, many of these counselors—especially those who feigned being lawyers—promised their clients work authorization but never told them that they were, in fact, applying for political asylum in order to obtain work permits. For many years, INS regularly denied work permits to asylum applicants in New York even though INS regulations authorized their issue. Immigrants' rights organizations sued the INS and for a time in the early 1990s immigrants whose asylum applications lingered more than 90 days at INS without a decision could request work authorization while their cases pended; this delay was increased to 150 days in 1995. Both honest law practitioners and unscrupulous entrepreneurs took advantage of the 90-day loophole while it existed, taking advantage of INS' slow application processing to obtain work permits on behalf of their clients. But many of the less honorable counselors took little care in preparing the actual asylum applications; their work was often so careless and misguided that they virtually guaranteed a denial. When their applications were denied, Salvadorans then were placed in deportation proceedings even if they had never been caught by INS before. For many, asylum became a trap.

When Roberto left El Salvador, he was is a diminutive man in his mid-twenties. He grew up in a peasant family in central El Salvador and became active in a church group that ran an agricultural cooperative in El Salvador. Roberto fled his country in 1989 when several members of the group were killed and the priest was threatened by the military. Within two months of his arrival in the U.S. Roberto found himself jobless and homeless. He could not find a job because employers everywhere were demanding work permits. Desperate, he took a friend's advice and consulted an attorney. The attorney promised to get him a work permit, took down some basic personal information and charged Roberto $350. Within a couple of months he received a letter from the INS stating that his political asylum application had been denied; with it was another document which said that deportation proceedings were to be carried out against him. Roberto was shocked. He had evaded the INS while crossing the border but now he was going to be deported. Little did he know that the attorney who promised him a work permit actually filled out an application for political asylum using only Roberto's name and birth date. The rest of the information on the papers was fabricated without Roberto's knowledge. So, later when Roberto was called to the INS, he obediently showed up expecting to receive his work permit. Instead, the INS examiner conducted an asylum interview with him. Roberto was asked him questions about his life in El Salvador and when his answers did not match the answers on the asylum application his application was denied.

Roberto's story is one of the few that has an ultimate happy ending. He confided his predicament to me and I was able to obtain better legal assistance for him. Some time later, Roberto was granted political asylum and eventually he was able to become a permanent resident. The vast majority of Salvadorans who fell into the asylum trap like Roberto did not fare nearly as well. Some received their coveted work permits through asylum applications, but this benefit was more than offset by the consequences of having their cases denied later. As the number of asylum applications filed by Salvadorans soared during the final years of the 1980s, the denial rate remained firm: 97.4 percent. The inequity of this situation did not escape notice. Many organizations who worked with the Salvadorans and other populations who were fleeing repressive governments, such as Guatemalans and Haitians, protested that the INS did not judge asylum applications based on the evidence of individuals' persecution presented, but on politics. They mounted evidence to prove that people who fled from governments which were allied with the U.S. government had little or no chance of being granted refugee or asylum status because this would embarrass the U.S. government. In the mid-1980s, they filed suit against the government.

Temporary Protected Status

On December 19, 1990, the INS and several legal advocates for Central Americans arrived at a settlement of a five-year lawsuit against the government, *American Baptist Churches v. Thornburgh* (hereafter "ABC"). The essence of the class-action suit was the claim that the government had not "decided on the granting of political asylum in a neutral, non-political manner, as required by law [under the 1980 Refugee Act]" (*New York Times* December 20, 1990). The ABC agreement stipulated that any Salvadoran (or Guatemalan) whose asylum application had been denied would be given another chance. The INS set up a new asylum system with a specially trained corp of adjudicators who were supposed to judge cases equitably on their merits. In the two years following the ABC settlement, asylum approval rates for Salvadorans rose quite dramatically, from less than 3 percent to 25 percent. Finally, deportation proceedings were halted against those immigrants' whose cases had been denied.

The ABC settlement was preceded by a bill passed by Congress in October 1990 which provided for Salvadorans to receive Temporary Protected Status (TPS). The granting of TPS to Salvadorans culminated a decade-long lobbying effort by many individuals and groups. Temporary Protected Status signified that Salvadorans who had arrived in the U.S. by September 19, 1990 would be able to remain in the country and obtain work authorization for a limited time period. The idea was to provide them with a temporary safe haven until the civil war terminated. Nearly 200,000 Salvadorans applied. They were not the only immigrant group to be extended TPS; Kuwaitis, Lebanese and Liberians were also allowed to apply for similar reasons but they were charged application fees of only $50 while the Salvadorans had to pay $110 (later raised to $135). Initially, Salvadorans were granted 18 months of TPS; this program was extended several times until January 1, 1995 and renamed "Deferred Enforced Departure" (DED). President Clinton decided to terminate Salvadorans' TPS/DED at that time, claiming that Salvadorans no longer needed safe haven because the civil war in their homeland had ended in 1992.[2] During the same timeperiod, asylum regulations were tightened, making it more difficult for new applicants to win their cases.

The announcement that TPS/DED would end sent a shudder throughout El Salvador as well as the Salvadoran communities in the United States. It drove a stake of insecurity through the hearts of both immigrants and their families. I experienced their anxiety first hand. Whenever I visited informants on Long Island after the announcement, they would invariably ask me what I thought was going to happen. And when I conducted research in their home communities in March 1995, the first question people always asked me was, "Do you think that the U.S. government will deport the Salvadorans en masse after the end of TPS?" Their fear is genuine. The repatriation of hundreds of thousands of Salvadorans would surely undermine post-war reconstruction efforts. In the past decade or so, both the government of El Salvador and much of its population has become dependent upon the steady influx of remittances from the Salvadorans abroad. Estimates of the value of these remittances range from $400 to $600 million (Funkhouser 1991) to $700 million by the Salvadoran government (*New York Times* March 11, 1992) to $1 billion (Montes Mozo & Garcia Vásquez 1988). In any case, remittances are El Salvador's greatest source of hard currency, more valuable than any of its exports.

The importance of remittances to the stability of El Salvador's economy is of such magnitude that the Salvadoran government has repeatedly made efforts to influence U.S. policy towards its nationals. In 1987, for example, then-president Napoleon Duarte, a strong ally of the U.S., officially petitioned the Reagan Administration *not* to deport the huge numbers of Salvadorans who were ineligible for permanent

---

2. Salvadorans' work permits were extended through January 1996, however, as was the timeperiod for submitting new political asylum claims under the ABC settlement. The changes in deadlines have proved confusing for Salvadorans as well as their employers. Some employers fired immigrant employees as of January 1, 1995, misunderstanding that work authorization for them was extended.

residence under the legalization provisions of IRCA. Duarte argued that a mass deportation would so destabilize the country as to exacerbate the conflict and suffering of the civil war. Salvadorans also anticipated that they would be rounded up and sent home. The day after the legalization program under IRCA ended in May 1987, Hempstead, which is the mecca for Salvadorans on Long Island, became a ghost town. People were so afraid that they stayed home from work and refrained from shopping or any public activities. The post-IRCA era has not, in fact, been characterized by large numbers of deportations of Salvadorans, either on Long Island or elsewhere. This is primarily due to the expense of hiring INS agents to seek out undocumented immigrants; the deportation proceedings in court are also costly and time-consuming.

Salvadorans and their families at home are deeply fearful of what will happen to them without the protection of TPS. The fact that INS did not initiate mass deportations following the IRCA legalization program has not convinced them that this will not happen now. Families are divided by immigration status and consequently could be torn apart by deportations. Consider the Pacheco family; Yolanda Pacheco came to Long Island to join her mother. She left her husband, Edgar, and her son by her first marriage in El Salvador. About a year later, Edgar migrated and two years after him, Yolanda sent for her son. Yolanda and Edgar both arrived before September 19, 1990 and therefore qualified for TPS, but Yolanda's son arrived afterward and did not qualify. In 1992, they had a second son who was born in the U.S. and is therefore a U.S. citizen. Yolanda has applied for permanent residency through her job as a nanny but her lawyer has told her that her papers will take many years to come through. If her petition is successful, Yolanda, Edgar and Yolanda's older son will all get green cards. In the meantime, however, the son is undocumented and Yolanda and Edgar have lost their temporary status. Yolanda is paid off the books so her work permit is not essential (though she must show she pays taxes to get her green card), but Edgar works for a pool maintenance company which may fire him when his work authorization expires. The family's situation is precarious, even after seven years in the United States.

Life as an Undocumented Immigrant

Though the likelihood of being deported from the streets of Long Island is not great given legal procedures and the limited number of INS staff, to my informants the fear is very real, particularly when they have been in the U.S. only a short time. Salvadorans come from a country with an extremely long history of political and economic repression. The elite have maintained control over the majority of the population through the institutions of the police and the Armed Forces. This type of atmosphere has taught Salvadorans to acquiesce to authority figures—and anyone in a uniform represents such authority. Their ingrained fear of authority figures extends to uniformed officials in the United States, whether the uniformed person is a security guard, a police officer or an INS agent. Consequently, Salvadorans feel their vulnerability day in and day out—at least in their early greenhorn days. Luz Aguilar, a well-educated urban Salvadoran, found it difficult not to mistake police officers for immigration agents when she first immigrated. "I even thought sometimes that the police were Immigration and I would shake when I saw them," she told me. "Now it seems so ridiculous to think that I was afraid of them, but people tell you to beware. [I was afraid of the police] because I thought they were connected with Immigration...because, I don't know, I just thought that they would come and ask me for my documents...This is because they were uniformed...[and the uniformed person in El Salvador] represents repression. Somebody with a uniform comes up to the step of your door and you feel like you have no rights at all, not even to defend yourself, not even to say 'What did I do?,' or 'I didn't do it.'"

Another informant described her insecurity as an undocumented person in terms of the kind of pressure it imposes. "I know that at any moment, say on my job, [the INS] could grab me and then I'd have to pay [a bond] of $3000...So I have to work hard, hard, hard to earn money so that if I have to go I will take some money back with me to my country....A legal person doesn't have to do that; he doesn't have to think about anything because if he loses his job he can find another because he has papers. But with me, no." Undocumented immigrants, unlike people granted asylum or refugee status and in contrast to much popular opinion, qualify for almost no government benefits such as welfare, unemployment insurance, food stamps and so on. In times of need, they rely on each other or on private charities such as food banks and soup kitchens. This helps to explain their urgency in finding and keeping work. They have no safety net to fall back on; additionally, they have family in their homelands who are depending on them to send back money for their support. Much like Jesús Argueta, they feel driven to fulfill these minimal goals, often by taking great personal risks and making severe personal sacrifices.

Obtaining Counterfeit Documentation

In the years following IRCA's passage, the market in counterfeit documents, or what Salvadorans call "*chuecos*" exploded (*New York Times* February 19, 1992). Any type of document from a driver's license to a green card to a work permit became available for a price. In the late 1980s, immigrants could buy a social security card and a green card (the old, truly green version) for $60 in Manhattan, although these were poor quality reproductions. The social security cards lacked serial numbers on their backs and the green cards were even shoddier. On a couple of occasions I accompanied informants to solicit jobs where the only documents they presented were chuecos. The most memorable time was at a Roy Rogers fast food restaurant. The applicant was Fermin Euceda, a slight man in his forties with jet-black hair. He asked the manager in broken English if the restaurant was hiring; the response was, "Show me your papers." The heavy-set manager took one look at the Salvadoran applicant's documents and said matter-of-factly, "Come back when you get better cards." The quality of the counterfeiting has improved steadily over the years and for good reason. Employers must comply with IRCA regulations to verify the work authorization of their new hires. But they do not have to be experts in documents and need only check if the credentials appear to be bona fide; that is, if they are *prima facie* genuine.

In 1991, Jesús Argueta borrowed a fake temporary resident card (given to legalization applicants during a trial period before they qualify for permanent residency) from a friend. I examined the card against others I had seen and noticed that it was nearly identical to the genuine article except that the typeface used was clearer than the one used by INS. In 1995, Sonia Acevedo showed me the green card she had purchased by mail from Miami. It too was nearly perfect—the colors and numbers on both faces and even the INS hologram looked authentic. The counterfeiters made only one flaw, conspicuous to the careful examiner. They misspelled "U.S. Department of Justice" as "U.S. Department of Jurstice" on the top front of the card. Sonia said she paid $350 for this document but that it had only worked once, at McDonalds.

For Salvadorans on Long Island, buying chuecos has been a necessary evil. Not only do they cost precious money that they would rather have spent on their needy families at home, but counterfeiting and even carrying counterfeit documents is a federal crime. Fearful that if they do not carry some identification on their person they risk deportation by the INS, undocumented Salvadorans tend to carry at least some of these phony cards in their wallets. Several times this has proven nearly ruinous. Jesús was a passenger in a car stopped by police in a routine investigation. When asked by the officers to produce identification, Jesús and the others obliged and were booked for possession of forged documents, a felony. It took months for this case to be resolved, costing Jesús numerous days of work. Jesús viewed this as a setback, not a defeat; he had traveled to far, risked too much, and had too many people depending on him, to fail.

2

Salvadorans Flee the Civil War

The civil war in El Salvador which raged from 1979 to 1992 put an end to Don José's career. A tall, thin man in his fifties with greying temples and spectacles perched atop his well-bridged nose, Don José owned a general store in a small city in Usulatán department where he sold a variety of goods and was able to live a comfortable life with his wife and young son. Before the war, he says, "we had a business that was doing very well." "We started the business with some credit but at that time if you asked for 50-70,000 *colones* [Salvadoran currency] in credit you could easily get it and repay it. I used to place orders for Christmas in November, taking a loan for up to 70,000 colones and on December 26 I would have paid off the entire loan. When the war started I would order in November and have to pay back the loan in December but I couldn't pay off the loan until May of the next year, some five to six months longer than before."

The war choked off his business because martial law and curfews were decreed; people could not go outside after dusk and they had little money to spend on basic goods, let alone enjoying themselves. "No one went out because they were afraid...The violence affected the economy and social life a lot," Don José explained to me. When the war began, "you had to be inside your house after six in the evening and not poke your nose outside because martial law was in effect.

Under martial law if anyone was outside the house after that hour they [the soldiers] would machine gun them like animals." The decline in his business was also hastened by government corruption (which required him to pay off bureaucrats to get permits for orders) and "war taxes" imposed by the anti-government guerrillas. These taxes were levied against all types of businesses and individuals and used to support the guerrillas. If the taxes were not paid, people were threatened with assassination or with the destruction of their establishments and homes.

Don José was forced to close his store, but the loss of his business did not convince him to come to the United States. He left El Salvador in 1988 only after a close friend and fellow entrepreneur was besieged and slain by guerrillas. According to José, "One day [the guerrillas] laid in wait for him until he got to a bridge. They found him, they killed him, they machine-gunned him and afterward they left him in his truck, poured gasoline on the truck, lit it and burned him inside the truck. That day I just happened to have sent my truck with another driver...and he was traveling about one kilometer behind my friend's truck. They say that when my driver turned a curve he saw the truck incinerated and ugh! He was startled and he shoved the truck into reverse and hightailed it back. He was almost crazy when he got back. My driver also came here to the United States." Don José interpreted this killing as a warning to himself because he, like the dead man, had been helping peasants with his truck by transporting them and their possessions out of areas of conflict. "Because of my business people would come by and say, 'Look, Don José, please do me this favor to take me away from here because I can't stand it anymore. They're going to kill me. I'll pay you whatever.'...I made about 17 trips for these people and the animals and furniture they took with them. One day the guerrillas sent a message to me through a peasant that they were waiting for me." But Don José did not heed the threat until his close friend was killed. After the killing, he obeyed the warning and left for the U.S.

When I asked Don José what motivated him to come to the U.S. he made no reference to his economic losses nor to any longstanding desire to visit. His response was simple:

"The only goal I hoped to find here was peace...The pressures of the war made life worthless over there [in El Salvador]. It takes only one jealous person or some bad person to point you out as having belonged to [the guerrillas or military]— even when you have never belonged—and [the military] go looking for you and to kill you. No, you can't live like that." Within a short time, Don José abandoned a life of privilege in El Salvador—a large home with servants and a handsome income from a highly respected occupation—for a single bed in an overcrowded, mildewy apartment and a job as an undocumented construction worker on Long Island. Despite his fall from grace, José is always referred to as "Don" by fellow Salvadorans, a term denoting high class status normally accorded to store owners, large landholders, and government officials. He also exudes a degree of refinement. He is always impeccably dressed and his hair remains slicked back in wavy curves along his head.

THE ROOTS OF THE WAR

During El Salvador's civil war an estimated 70,000 people were killed—approximately one in every 100 Salvadorans. An estimated one million more fled the country entirely and resettled in other countries, mostly in the United States. Yet another one million were displaced from their homes and forced to move elsewhere in El Salvador. Prior to the conflict only a trickle of Salvadorans had migrated to the United States; most people had never even contemplated visiting. It took a bloodbath to convince them to leave, to "save their scalps" as Yolanda told me. The war left virtually no family untouched. It is recalled not only for its immense impact but for its ferocity as well. Victims were not only killed, but slain after they had been taken forcibly from their homes, tortured (including the rape of women), and disfigured. Dismembered bodies appeared in the mornings, left in the public view as a clear warning to all that dissidents would share the same fate. Many scholars and social commentators have tried to understand the roots of this brutality much as generations of researchers have endeavored to comprehend how people could create the Holocaust. A full discussion of their

viewpoints and findings lies beyond the scope of this book
(see Armstrong & Shenk 1982; Barry 1987; Bulmer-Thomas
1987; Dunkerely 1988; Pearce 1986; LaFeber 1983). What I
will provide here is an overview and synthesis of the history
leading up to the war and then present my informants' eye-
witness accounts of it. I concentrate on their testimonies because relatively little firsthand evidence has been published
on what the war was like and because the testimonies provide a personal dimension that is essential to grasping the
intensity and barbarity of the war.

Most scholars agree that the principal pressure leading up
to civil warfare was deep-seated social and economic inequalities. The origin of these inequalities dates back at least to
Central America's colonization by the Spaniards in the six-
teenth century. The original colonists came to the region looking for gold but, finding little, turned to planting indigo [a
blue dye] and cocoa and producing meat for export back to
the Old World (Woodward 1985; Wolf 1959; Pearce 1986;
Hawkins 1984). The indigenous peoples, the Maya and Pipil
Indians, were dispossessed of their lands, forced to labor for
the colonists and many perished from exploitation and Euro-
pean diseases. This set in motion a two-tiered class system
where the colonists dominated and the indigenous population was deemed inferior and subhuman.

When Central America broke away from Spain in the
1800s and individual nation-states were formed, the elites
began a neo-colonial dependency on export commodities,
particularly coffee (Woodward 1985). By this time, much of
the Salvadoran population consisted of mestizo peasants,
poor farmers of mixed ancestry. They planted on common
lands, a vestige of the colonial land distribution system which
granted most land to elites and ceded little for use in common
by the workers as pasturelands and for raising their own subsistence crops.

In the late nineteenth century, a coffee fever swept
through Central America. To increase lands available for coffee production, the government of El Salvador passed a de-
cree in 1881 which privatized the common lands (Armstrong
and Schenk 1982). The best soil for coffee production in El Salvador lay in the western third of the country, a mountainous

zone with rich volcanic earth and high altitudes suited to coffee trees. Peasants living on these lands were pushed off; some became *colonos* or laborers on the large farms and others migrated to poorer lands to the east. This displacement of the peasantry and consolidation of productive lands in the hands of a small coffee oligarchy accelerated throughout the twentieth century, reaching a peak in the 1970s and 1980s. By then four percent of all the farms accounted for 60 percent of the lands used for coffee production and they were owned by 36 families (Barry 1987:26-7). For example, in 1975, 41 percent of El Salvador's peasantry was landless (Hamilton and Chinchilla 1991:90).

Starting in the mid-twentieth century, other commodities for export were planted including cotton, sugar and beef. This further exacerbated landlessness and poverty. The dispossessed poor responded moving to marginal land areas, intensifying agricultural production, supplementing subsistence agriculture through seasonal migration to harvest export commodities, and emigrating to neighboring Honduras until the Soccer War of 1969 between Honduras and El Salvador forced them to return. In addition, many migrated to the cities and some city dwellers began to migrate to the United States, as well as other countries, from the 1960s onward (see Mahler 1992 for a longer discussion).

During the 1960s and 1970s El Salvador promoted industrialization, but there were never enough jobs to meet demand and wages were very low. Twenty percent of urban households earned an income below minimum subsistence (Deere & Driskin 1984:32 cited in Pearce 1986:33). In the 1970s, other events including the 1973 oil embargo which sent inflation spiralling upward, a sharp drop in the world coffee price in 1978 and 1979, and a failed attempt at land tenure reform sharpened economic and social tensions in the country. In these years many rural and urban organizations were formed to work for reform and radical change. They ranged from church groups and unions to student alliances and guerrilla factions. They became organized into a collective opposition, the FDR-FMLN, only after the country was plunged into outright civil war in 1979 following a military coup and the downfall of a moderate civilian and military government. FDR stands for Frente Democrático Revolucionario or Democratic Revolutionary Front, formed in April 1980 as a moderate to left-wing political and diplomatic organization. The FMLN or Farabundo Martí National Liberation Front is the collective label for some five guerrilla factions which coalesced in November 1980. (See Armstrong and Shenk [1982] for details.) The FDR-FMLN represents one side, or *bando* as Salvadorans say, of the conflict and the Salvadoran Armed Forces (including police units, the National Guard and the army) represent the other.

The Salvadoran Armed Forces, particularly the National Guard (a special rural security force), have been a major force in El Salvador since they brutally repressed a peasant rebellion in 1932. Historically, 1932 had two major impacts. The first was the virtual extinction of popular protest, a death knell that would last for nearly five decades (Anderson 1971). The second impact was the shift in power to favor the Armed Forces at the expense of the oligarchy, a trend which would accelerate with time. "For the wealthy, 1932 was the dark night of their worst fears. Henceforth, the oligarchy would cede the responsibility for governing El Salvador to the Armed Forces." (Armstrong & Shenk 1982:30). The Armed Forces became one of the only institutions in El Salvador which offered social mobility by providing education and training to children of peasants. From the 1960s through the 1980s, however, economic and military aid, primarily from the United States, fueled widespread corruption within the Armed Forces, which appropriated much of the aid for themselves (Millman 1989). Moreover, the military came to view themselves as superior to the elites as well as the peasants and operated with impunity. Don José terms this attitude *prepotencia militar*. "Prepotencia means power," he explained, "which is supreme over all citizens. That is, if I am from the military then I have the authority to take someone from his home in the night and kill him. And I make out a report of the incident showing that he opposed me or tried to kill me and I had to kill him. Or I make him out to be a guerrilla. The military is all-powerful, in the city it is all-powerful and no one in the country can touch them. They can do exactly what they want to...The *militares* do exactly what they want; they have killed people, they've massacred people, they've orchestrated all of the *vejamenes* [troubles] that have occurred in the country. And this is not just today but since before the war. The war blew up because of them, because of their prepotencia. Because they can do whatever they want."

Civil warfare lasted a dozen years and 70,000 people died, most of them civilians who were often slain after being tortured. Despite enormous human and economic losses, neither side could win the war. In 1991, peace talks began between the FMLN and the Salvadoran government and were mediated by the United Nations. In early 1992 a peace accord was signed followed by a cease-fire. The FMLN was promised land for its ex-combatants and the right to participate as a political party in upcoming elections. They disbanded and destroyed their arms. The United Nations stayed for three more years to assure peace and left at the end of April 1995. But while the war has ended, inequalities and violence remain. Few land titles to the FMLN have been given out and there is extensive discontent among decommissioned soldiers. They are widely associated with a crime wave that has struck in peacetime, responsible for thousands of murders and robberies committed in 1994—a level commensurate with the violence during the war. People I spoke to in El Salvador invariably remarked that the violence was worse in 1995 than before the end of the war because it had become so unpredictable. During the war, people learned how to avoid much of the conflict by keeping quiet and avoiding certain areas. But recent assaults appear to be much more random, occurring in broad daylight and sparing virtually no one.

The United States' Role in the War

The United States supported the Salvadoran government as an ally during the entire civil war. Over one billion dollars of military and economic aid were funneled to El Salvador during this period. The U.S. government also trained Salvadoran soldiers and commanders both within El Salvador and the United States. The political policy behind this U.S. aid was containment, keeping the leftist guerrillas from assuming power and establishing a Marxist regime in the U.S. sphere of influence. In short, the policy was to prevent another Cuba, to prevent the assumption of power by any regime that might threaten U.S. interests in Central America. This approach was voiced by Thomas Enders, Secretary of State under President Ronald Reagan, in a statement to the House Sub-Committee on Inter-American Affairs on February 2, 1982. "There is no mistaking that the decisive battle for Central America is underway in El Salvador. If, after Nicaragua, El Salvador is captured by a violent minority, who in Central America would not live in fear? How long would it be before major US strategic interests—the canal, sealanes, oil supplies—were at risk?" (cited in Dunkerley 1988:335).

This international policy affected domestic policy regarding Salvadorans who fled the war and entered U.S. territory illegally. The U.S. government refused to view them as bona fide political refugees and labeled them "economic" migrants. President Reagan was the main architect of this practice, resolving to keep Central Americans, whom he termed "feet people," from "swarming into our country seeking a safe haven" (Loescher & Scanlan 1986:192). In fact, political factors are the underlying cause of the massive movement of Salvadorans to the U.S. True, Salvadoran immigrants hope for better economic opportunities here, but it was the political and economic instability caused by the war that propelled so many to leave their homeland. In sum, Salvadorans were extremely poor before the civil war, but very few emigrated to the United States before 1979. Poverty did not drive them to flee, fear for their lives did.

THE IMPACT OF THE CIVIL WAR

The war played a critical role in the lives of Salvadoran immigrants, but what were their lives like before the conflict? And how did their lives change as a consequence of the war? These are difficult questions to answer because Salvadorans' recollections, especially of their lives before the war, are often tinged with romanticism and nostalgia; they are reconstructions much as this book is my reconstruction of their experiences. Their accounts do offer insights into the way things were, which is particularly important since here is no full-fledged ethnography of rural or urban Salvadoran life prior to 1979.

Life Before the War

El Salvador has been and continues to be a country with an agricultural soul. Most of its population still lives in rural areas or is only one generation removed from a peasant life style. Regardless of location, daily life in El Salvador revolves around family, work and religion. People live close to relatives and social relations are dense. Nowhere is this more true than in the tiny hamlets, the *caseríos*. These are the smallest residential units in the countryside, usually no larger than a few dozen homes which knit together several extended families. Hamlets are dispersed within municipalities or *cantones* and are isolated from one another as well as rural towns by the country's topography. Land in El Salvador is extremely irregular. Much of it is covered by rugged mountains interspersed with volcanoes and volcanic plains, but even outside these striking features the land is very hilly and craggy. Only along the Pacific ocean is the land flat but this is a very small percentage of the entire surface of the country. Consequently, caseríos are often located on the tops of hills or in valleys, connected by paths and less frequently by roads. Transportation is an ever-present problem making most areas inaccessible by car or even four-wheel drive vehicles. In order to get from the caseríos in to small towns, people ride horses or walk to a road where they can find better transportation.

The geographic isolation and kinship ties of the caseríos foster very tight social ties. Most peasants who live in these hamlets are small-time farmers who sow corn, beans, and millet to feed themselves and their few livestock. Women and children remain tied to the home where the day begins before dawn with the preparation of tortillas for breakfast. Children go to a one-room school for a half day of instruction and then return home for lunch. They assist the family by gathering firewood and fruits from trees near their homes, hauling water for washing, and helping to prepare meals. They also tend to the family's animals: they chase the chickens who run freely in and out of the houses made out of dried mud with dirt floors; they also milk the cows and saddle the horses if the family is fortunate enough to have these larger animals. Men and older male children leave early for the fields, particularly in the growing season between May and August. If they are lucky enough to have several acres of land that is not too dry or vertical, a family will usually produce enough food to feed itself but often have little or none left over to sell. Many families own no land and must rent fields or work as day laborers who plant and harvest the crops of larger land-holders for wages.

Sister Maria Villatoro's family was one of the many who owned no land. As a child, she, her father, and several of her siblings worked on farms owned by large landholders, earning wages for harvesting coffee. The money she brought in was valuable to her family so she had to stop attending school after a year or two, only becoming educated as an adult when she decided to become a nun. "We grew up poor, very poor. We only had enough to eat and clothe ourselves—the most basic necessities." Since her family produced no food of their own, they had to buy it as well as other goods which made them worse off than families with at least some land to sow. "We had to buy everything, everything. I remember that sometimes my mother didn't have anything to give us to eat and we would go and look for berries and other plants and my mother would cook them in water with salt and we wouldn't have anything else to eat...I remember seeing tears fall from my mother's eyes when she would say, 'Ay! my daughter! You are going to have to live with this; it's all I have to give to you.'"

The material deprivation of peasant life was compensated by its rich social ties. In times of need, for instance, people could solicit help from family and friends within the caserío and this aid was almost always forthcoming. Sister Maria, like many of my peasant informants, recalled this fondly. "It was a very small village where we lived. Everyone knew each other. Over there, a person's problems were shared with the rest. It was a community." In my country " if you don't have anything then you go next door and say, 'Señora so-and-so, don't you have some beans you could give me so I can eat them with tortillas?'" What Maria is describing is what anthropologists refer to as reciprocity. In peasant life there is little economic security because a drought or other natural catastrophe can destroy one's crops. This insecurity is counterbalanced by exchanges between families, people knitted together by kinship and friendship ties, such that resources get distributed quite evenly. I witnessed this daily during my research in El Salvador. Women would gather eggs or fruits in the morning and have children take some of them to a mother-in-law or a *comadre* (a fictive kin member created through baptism of children. Godparents of a child become *compadres* of the child's parents.). Visitors, even if they were just next-door neighbors, were always offered a *refresco* or cool juice drink and when a family hosted a religious service in their home (since churches were usually a long distance away), they provided food for dozens of congregants.

Regardless of landownership status, rural Salvadorans always need some cash income to buy clothes, tools, school supplies, fertilizer, medicines and medical treatment and other necessities. Until the civil war began, they earned this cash largely by working part of the year on coffee, cotton, or sugar plantations. Jesús explained to me the economics of the peasantry. "Most don't produce enough to cover their expenses and nothing is left over for clothes. That's why we went to the *cortas* [coffee harvests] because for most people what they produce is not even enough to eat from." A Salvadoran sociologist who was murdered by the military during the war, Segundo Montes (1986), found that on average 40 percent of rural families sent one or more members to the coffee harvests every year. In sum, peasants combined several types of income and resource distribution to eke out an existence. They produced some if not most of their own food, they sold some goods in the market for money, they earned wages to buy necessities they could not produce and they shared resources with each other. As I shall illustrate shortly, this delicate balance was completely upset during the war, driving hundreds of thousands of peasants out of their rural homes. They became laborers in the burgeoning cities, in the United

States and in other countries, remitting monies home to their families.

Fewer Salvadorans on Long Island had grown up in El Salvador's towns and cities than in the rural cantones, making it hard for me to provide a composite picture of the urban life style. Moreover, in the urban areas social class is more varied. Whereas in the country, class lines are very rigid between poor peasants and wealthy large landowners, in the cities and particularly in San Salvador, the capital city, there are more intermediary layers: workers, students, and middle-class bureaucrats, and entrepreneurs. A few of the Salvadorans I interviewed were university students or people with high levels of training. Yolanda was an officeworker who studied in the university at night; Elena Turcios finished school and began to organize the poor in San Salvador's neighborhoods on behalf of the poor; and Ernesto Reyes attended industrial engineering classes at the national university in San Salvador at night while working in an aluminum and glass factory by day. He never finished his degree, though he studied for a decade, because the government shut down the university several times and for long periods, claiming that it was a breeding ground for subversives. During the 1960s and 1970s, the country industrialized and service firms grew larger, absorbing some of the rural to urban migrants. The rest worked in the burgeoning informal economy as food vendors, domestics, and day laborers. Edgar was born in San Vicente department but at an early age moved to San Salvador where he learned the shoemaker trade and lived in a *mesón* with his uncle. Until recent years, many urban poor lived in *mesones*. These are single-story rectangular structures with a central area for public use. People rent rooms along the perimeter and share cooking, cleaning and hygienic facilities. Children play freely in the common while women attend to chores. Rents are inexpensive compared to other types of housing in the cities but are still burdensome to recent migrant families who were not used to paying rent in the caseríos.

Religion is extremely important in Salvadoran life. Until the past decade or so, nearly the entire population was Catholic. Priests travel constantly, often performing several masses in different towns within their jurisdiction each Sunday. In the rural areas, it is impossible for most priests to reach every community weekly; mass is often led by a cleric only once a month. The rest of the time local leaders or catechists conduct worship and provide religious education to the children. Despite the informality, Christian belief and tradition are profoundly rooted. One nun on Long Island described Salvadorans as possessing a "simple but deep faith." Daily conversations are punctuated with phrases such as "If God wills" and "God will repay you." In recent years, Protestant evangelical churches, most notably the Apostles and Prophets Church and the Pentecostal denominations, have won many converts. The success of evangelical churches is particularly striking in the remote, rural areas bordering Honduras. Here many evangelical women readily identify their faith by covering their heads with lace scarves. Often families are divided by faith, some remaining Catholic while others convert to Protestantism. This is also true on Long Island where there are several evangelical churches headed by Salvadorans. I have heard varying opinions regarding this schism. Some people believe that it has not affected family relations while others claim that it has caused friction. The evangelicals are very tightly-knit on Long Island and very dedicated to their sister churches in their homeland. One congregation in Gold coast collected funds to build a large Apostles and Prophets church in their home town several years ago; they recently funded the building of a road to the church from town and the installation of electricity to the area. Meanwhile, the Catholic church on Long Island has responded slowly to the arrival of Salvadoran parishioners. Most Catholic churches on the island were created for Irish or Italian congregations and, if they offer services in Spanish, they are nonetheless dominated by older Latino migrants from Puerto Rico and South America.

Life Under Civil Warfare

If life before the civil war was difficult, it was much worse afterwards. Tensions in El Salvador escalated in the 1970s as did repression of reformers. In the cities, death squads appeared and targeted labor and political leaders. Often these victims would be delivered *anónimos* or anonymous notes stating that they would be killed if they continued their activities. Hours or days later armed and masked men would enter their homes and, in front of their families, take them away to be tortured and killed. Women were raped and then killed. In the countryside a key institution carrying out this repression was the Civil Defense. The Civil Defense (CD) was a rural paramilitary police force comprised of commanders who led a group of peasant recruits. The CD was an efficient means of placing more men under military control without expanding the army. But it came to be widely associated with violent crimes against the peasantry *prior* to the appearance of the guerrilla forces. "The injustices that the National Guard committed were done for the oligarchy, the rich," Teofilo Gómez insisted. Teofilo was a lay priest in La Unión department and was often sought by the families of victims for consolation and advice. "For instance, there were cattlemen where I lived. So...in order to kill off a worker or peasant who [the elite] didn't like or who had done something against their will, they'd give money to the Guard to kill him." When I asked Teofilo whether this was a common practice, he said, "Yes, it was very common. There was a lot of corruption, not only in the government but everywhere. For example, the rich in the town could order someone to be killed just because he was *Don Fulano de tal* [Mr. so-and-so]. Someone would talk to the Guard and say so-and-so did something against me, he robbed me—even though it was a lie—and the Guard would kill him; they'd torture him, they'd imprison him, torture him and then kill him." Teofilo's testimony documents how class cleavages and even personal differences became the justification for many early atrocities. Rape, murder, torture, kidnappings and ransomings became even more commonplace than before and there was no way to safeguard oneself from the terror. The violence was particularly pronounced in the eastern departments of Morazán and La Unión where most of the Long Island Salvadorans are from.

Santos Rosa's story contains themes found in almost every account I collected: false accusations, revenge, and the persecution of the innocent by guerrillas and military alike. Santos is an illiterate, landless peasant in his late thirties from Morazán department. This area was one of the most embattled and its lands are some of the poorest in the country. He has a wife and seven children, ranging in age from thirteen to two years whom he supported by working as a *jornalero* or day laborer on others' farms and by going to the coffee harvest in Santa Ana or Sonsonate departments each year. While harvesting, he said, "You sleep like a dog. In the U.S. even the dogs sleep better than we did there. Sometimes you got food but mostly just two tortillas and a spoonful of beans." In 1981 he took a bus to the harvest but when it came close to the capital city of San Salvador dozens of shots rang out. Peeking out of the bus he saw that the streets were covered with "body parts," one torso was cut completely in half and blood ran down the street. The experience so frightened him that he stopped picking coffee that year; his family would have to make do with less.

Life was no less hazardous for Santos in Morazán. Even simple daily chores like carrying food were deemed subversive, he said, because you would be accused by the military of working as a *mula* [pack-horse] for the guerrillas. "The most you could carry with you were two *arrobas* [25 pound bags] of corn, one of rice, one of sugar and one of beans...If you had more than that, if you had a *carga* [sack] of corn they took it away from you. If they found batteries on you they'd take them away too, because they would say that you were doing business with the guerrillas....Then what they would do was take away your *cedula* [national identification card], tie your hands behind you, blindfold you and take your money from you."

The military was not the only source of peasant repression. The guerrillas played their part as well. Peasants who, through hard work, were able to get a bit ahead were often the first victims of the guerrillas and there was no way to denounce the abuse. "We were three brothers and we had seven cows," Santos recalled, "and we had the idea that we could sell the cows and buy some land to build a house on...We were renting at the time. When it came time to sell the cows the guerrillas arrived. All the capital that we had was taken by the guerrillas...We couldn't do anything because...if we reported it to the military they would accuse us of being with the guerrillas." Santos says that the guerrillas occupied his town for four years and during that time they took all the cattle from the peasants as well as all their other animals. While he speaks bitterly about the guerrillas, he is equally bitter about the soldiers who bombed and machine-gunned the town several times. He also recalls the death squads, stating that you could not show that you were nervous in front of them; if you started begging for mercy, you would be killed. That is why the death squads were, as he says, "the godless ones."

Santos' most bitter memory is of a man who pretended to be with the guerrillas but, in actuality, was not. This man would circulate among the peasantry demanding "war taxes" or payoffs in exchange for being left alone. Several times he went to Santos' house looking for him but he was harvesting corn in neighboring Honduras. A couple of months after Santos returned to El Salvador, the man reappeared at his door demanding money. "When he came into the room," Santos continued, "we pulled a machete on him [and scared him away]. The guerrillas found out what happened because this man had a brother in the guerrillas and they came back looking for me. It was during that same month that I fled to Honduras." He stayed there long enough to earn some money to emigrate to the U.S. in 1989.

Santos' experience highlights how difficult it became for peasants to survive in the violent climate of the 1980s. Santos' attempts at earning a living through day labor, seasonal labor and even international labor migration to nearby Honduras were thwarted by the war. Margarita Cáceres grew up in the town of Nueva Esparta in La Unión department. She was fortunate because her family could afford to send her to high school to become a teacher; there were no high school programs in her town, so she had to travel two hours by bus to the city of San Miguel. After graduation, she began studying for an associate's degree in accounting, but in 1981 Margarita's parents urged her to leave El Salvador for the United States because the guerrillas were recruiting educated youth as teachers to give classes in their camps. What Margarita remembers most is the carnage that she saw every day as she took the bus to school. "Things had already gotten bad as of 1975 and 1976. But by 1980 it had become too much. If you left my town to go to the city, you would encounter dead bodies everywhere on the edge of the streets...You couldn't recognize the people because oftentimes there would only be body parts. Heads were placed on the stakes used to make fences."

The images Edgar witnessed from his shoe workshop in San Salvador were equally if not more horrifying. "Imagine, a pick-up truck [that is normally used to carry firewood]. But on this occasion it wasn't carrying firewood. It was cadavers, half-destroyed cadavers. Imagine adolescents, boys between 14 and 21 years old, half-mutilated with only half of their faces left. Some were naked. Others only had on their underwear. Women in their panties only. Women without bras on and with bullet wounds in their breasts. Imagine, imagine what a sight—so ugly, so *turbe* as we say. You are working but your mind is thinking that next door is a funeral parlor and that over there they are preparing all those cadavers...Really, it's an unimaginable situation." During this time it was nearly impossible to exact justice for these crimes. Some brave women formed a group called CoMadres, a group of mothers and sisters of the disappeared and murdered who denounced these acts to the government and internationally (Schirmer 1993).

Most Salvadorans so feared retribution by either the guerrillas or the military if they voiced their grievances that they remained quiet, a strategy of professed neutrality. Even today, Salvadorans say that they emigrated "because of *la situación,*" because of the situation. "*La situación*" is a euphemism for the civil war, a simple word which gives the listener virtually no idea what people endured. It is one of many obfuscations adopted by Salvadorans in their quest to appear neutral, to show no favoritism or links to either the guerrillas or the Armed Forces. To take sides in any way was to invite denouncements and retaliation. "The people could favor neither side, not even think about leaning towards one side. They had to stay in the middle," Nicolás Guzmán told me. "Because if they sided with one group then they would die, they'd be killed. So, they had to be really calm, *tranquilo.*"

Nicolás was a child when the war broke out in a canton out-side his hometown of Polorós. His older brothers fled the country early and then sent for him when he became a teen-ager, an age when the youth were at high risk of being forc-ibly recruited into either the military or the guerrillas.

Fear of involuntary conscription plagued boys from the tender age of thirteen (in violation of international law) to men as old as in their forties (Americas Watch 1987). While I was in El Salvador, parents told me they started sending their male children abroad in record numbers when both sides began stopping vehicles traveling along the roads in order to pull men off and take them away to be trained. Not only did the threat of recruitment spur emigration but so did actual service. Men who served in the military had their national identity cards or *cédulas* marked as veterans. These became flags to guerrillas when they stopped individuals and de-manded to see their papers. Cándido Cruz told me that after he left the army he got a new cédula which had no record of his military service because, "Ah! If [the guerrillas] found it marked on your cedula that you've served, then they'd take you away to kill you or force you to join them." Cándido is a landless peasant in his forties, also from La Unión depart-ment, who joined the army in order to provide a stable in-come for his family. Once Cándido finished his term, however, he found that he could no longer go back home. He fled to the U.S. instead.

The guerrillas viewed past military service as a threat since those who had served could be recalled into service from the reserves. "They told me, 'Better we kill you than have you in the army,'" Lorenzo Ramos said of the guerrillas. A young man in his early twenties, Lorenzo had a promising construction career on the outskirts of the city of San Miguel in eastern El Salvador. "Once I served in the army I was a con-demned man," he recalled. "Once you have been in the mili-tary, or if you've fought the guerrillas, you have problems. Each side has its spies and they know you. Because of this, I said, 'It's better for me to leave [the country] because they could come and take me away.' Anyone could point the fin-ger at someone, at you, say that you were a soldier, that you fought against him [and you could be killed]. For this reason I [left the country]."

Men were not the only ones who suffered under forced recruitment. It was a constant source of anxiety to women as well. Yolanda fretted about her husband Edgar and her brother each day they left the house to go to work. She, like countless wives and mothers, never knew if they would return. "You can be in your neighborhood," she explained, "and see that a truck has pulled up and has started to recruit and what the military does is wait for the youth to return to their houses from work. They catch them when they get off the buses coming home from work so that their own communities don't find out that they have been taken off. So what you have to do is get very close to the truck and watch to make sure that no one that you know has been taken and, if so, to see what you can do to get them out. They take them and then they don't give them enough training before they send them to the front lines and they come home with their legs mutilated because they haven't gotten enough training to know how to defend themselves. And this is something that you have to be constantly worried about. In my case, I would come home from work and would hear that they were recruiting nearby and I would run out of the house fearful for my brother and husband. When I would meet one of them coming back I would say 'Thank God. Go back home and don't leave!' Then I'd go out again until I met the other and if it got late and I still hadn't met him I would start wringing my hands and thinking, 'What might have happened?' And I'd wait a little bit more and worry because they never tell you when they are going to recruit. It's really difficult, it tortures you psychologically. You're never at ease. When they leave the house you never know if they will return."

The war drastically affected people economically as well as emotionally. Livelihoods were destroyed. Often the devastation was swift and ruinous such as when villages were attacked. In Benjamín Velásquez's town in the northern department of Chalatenango, the guerrillas took over and would not let anyone leave. Benjamín and his family had been living there all their lives raising and selling cattle, and a few days after the guerrillas came, they had nothing. The guerrillas held the town for three days then left just before the soldiers arrived. The military, warning the townspeople that the guerrillas had retreated to the hills and would attack only by night, ordered an evacuation. "We fled with only our clothes and a few things," Benjamín recalled. "Everything else was left behind. There were eight days of fighting and since the day when we were driven away we have never returned to our home...When the fighting was over the military didn't allow anyone to go back to live." When I asked him what happened to the town he said, "Everything was burned, destroyed by the bombings. Fires and incendiary bombs destroyed almost all of the houses...After eight days I went back to see if we could salvage some of our things...It was tremendously disillusioning—the houses bombed out, everything burned...I found almost nothing left. The animals had died during the bombings too." Not too long afterward Benjamín left the country with money borrowed from a cousin already living in Houston, Texas. His family has never been able to return to their old farm in Chalatenango.

Economic devastation for most Salvadorans was more prolonged than for Benjamín and his family. During the war agricultural and industrial production fell dramatically. Transportation was a key factor in this decline because it was so dangerous; people could neither get themselves to work nor their products to market. Companies began to fail as incomes fell and people could not afford to buy more than the bare essentials. "When I started to work at one factory," explained Yolanda, "the sales were good, the profits were good. The products were always sold because salesmen could motivate the people to buy them. But now the salesmen couldn't get advances from the factories because people were too afraid to buy and so nothing was sold. This was due to the war...Thus, there was no money coming into the companies and they went under and this affected the workers who were dependent upon our salaries." Much as in Don José's case, many owners of companies and small businesses were made to pay "war taxes" which siphoned off their profits and discouraged business. Seasonal migrations to harvest coffee and other export commodities also became too dangerous, further depleting the buying power of the peasantry. In the countryside, the guerrillas exacted war taxes from the peasants and shopkeepers; if people did not comply they were threatened with death or involuntary collaboration. Jesús paid war taxes for years until it was economically impossible. Thereafter, the guerrillas forced him to pay his taxes in labor and he began work as a "mule" transporting food to the guerrilla camps at night. For over a year he went virtually without sleep because during the day he had to work his own land and at night he had to carry heavy cargoes for the guerrillas. This ruined his health and carried the risk that his collusion, although involuntary, would be discovered.

The Armed Forces and the guerrillas also depleted people's resources by demanding food. Sometimes they demanded whole sacks of corn and other staples or livestock. Other times, they would pass through a village demanding that the people prepare them food. "There were occasions when a half hour after the military left the guerrillas would come by," explained Teofilo, the lay priest. "The guerrillas would come by and say, 'How are you Father? How is everything?' And I would say, 'And how are you?...and the guerrilla commander would ask me, 'Have the enemy come by?' I had to learn new words [to call the military] with them. 'Those dogs,' I'd say because I had to get along with them. You had to adapt yourself to the atmosphere. 'How are those dogs? Those dogs are afraid of you!' I'd say. 'Truly they haven't come?' he'd ask. "No,' I'd tell him. Then he'd say, 'Father, give me a cup of coffee.' 'Of course,' I'd respond, 'sit down.' 'Did you have anything to eat?' 'No.' So I'd prepare eggs, tortillas and so on. And about a half hour after the guerrillas had left, the army would arrive and it would start all over again. 'Hello Father. How are you doing? Do you have any fresh water? And Father, have you seen the guerrillas?' And I'd have to say, "No. Those dogs haven't passed through here.' And of course they had just been with me! And this is what happened all the time. Ay!" Teofilo's experience was reiterated over and over by other informants from the countryside; the constant fear and imposition turned them against both sides of the conflict. During the war agricultural production fell making it difficult for people to feed their own families, let alone legions of combatants. But if they did not comply with the bandos' demands they would pay a price, often with their lives.

Key Events of the Civil War

The civil war in El Salvador was punctuated by several key events which received widespread international recognition. They left deep impressions on Salvadorans who lived through them. Two of the most significant incidents were the 1980 murder of Archbishop Oscar Arnulfo Romero and the 1989 guerrilla offensive. Oscar Romero had been a relatively conservative Catholic priest during the 1970s when several clerics and some parishes became directly involved in organizing the poor for their rights. After one of these priests, his close friend Father Rutilio Grande, was murdered, Romero began to speak out frequently against death squads which were associated with the country's far right. He was gunned down on March 24, 1980 while saying mass in San Salvador. Several days later thousands attended his funeral and were bombed and strafed by the military, leaving 26 dead and two hundred wounded (Armstrong and Shenk 1982:151). Edgar was present when the shooting erupted. "The day that Monsignor Romero was buried I was working," he recalled. "After the funeral there was some shooting. People started fleeing. A youth got close to me and was at a corner looking back and there were some sharp shooters in the building. The kid stuck his head out and he was hit by a bullet. He jumped up and fell and there he stayed. We went out from the workshop to see him, we saw that his brains were spilling out of the back of his head as if a coconut had been split open. His skull was destroyed as if it had been broken into little pieces. The back of his skull was completely open. A pregnant woman came by to identify him. It was his wife; this guy had been married only six months. But before she arrived, a whole group of people fled from the demonstration. One person stopped [a friend of his who had also been in the demonstration], held the body and cradled his head. Brains fell onto his hands and this person said, 'This is my people's blood.' He rested the body down and he put a handkerchief on him with UDN on it, for the Nationalist Democratic Union [one of the organizations on the left]."

Oscar Romero's murder and the bloodshed at his funeral were widely condemned but did not stem the violence. The fighting continued for years with no side gaining a clear advantage. In 1989, the FMLN guerrillas launched what they thought would be the final offensive of the war. The target this time was the cities, areas which had seen less direct fighting than the countryside. During the offensive in November, parts of the capital as well as much of the eastern city of San Miguel were taken over by the guerrillas, who were then counterattacked by the military. The result was the slaughter of civilians caught in the middle. For many people this round of violence destroyed their faith in a peaceful solution to El Salvador's crisis and they fled the country. Carmen Rivas was among those caught in the crossfire. At the time of the attack, Carmen was living in San Miguel with her two young children, her half sister and that sister's father. One night at about ten the guerrillas took over her neighborhood on the outskirts of the city. The occupation and ensuing bombing lasted ten days. She and her family spent the first days under their beds. During the bombing and strafing, many bullets struck the house; one hit her sister and another entered the older man's leg, but they couldn't seek medical treatment because the fighting was too intense. Carmen tells of feeding her toddlers sugar water for several days because there was no more food and because they could not leave the house. Shortly after the fighting died down, Carmen sent word to her husband, who was already on Long Island, asking him to finance her trip to the U.S., and when the money arrived she left. Carmen suffered from nervous attacks due to the bombing and shooting long after she arrived on Long Island. Her mother also became very ill, her nerves shattered, and sent word to Carmen that the children would frequently wake up at night screaming and crying.

To summarize the events leading up to the massive immigration of Salvadorans into the U.S. I will make two fundamental points. First, this migration was preceded by a long history of people being uprooted. They were displaced from the land needed to grow their crops, from the coffee harvests which had become their means to compensate for insufficient land, from Honduras where they sought new lands, and from their country as a consequence of warfare. Second, when they were driven away from their homeland, there were few places they could contemplate seeking refuge. Consider the dilemmas so many faced in the 1980s. They were penniless and illiterate; the only occupation they knew was tilling the soil and raising a family. But now there was no home to return to. They could move to a city but few jobs were available there and, unlike in the country where they had their own homes and produced their food, everything had to be purchased. In the city the war raged too, so that little protection could be found there. They could settle illegally in neighboring Nicaragua or Guatemala but those countries were in the midst of their own civil wars. And they, or their family members, may have been expelled from Honduras before, so they could not find refuge there. Mexico was a possibility but there was little work and the Mexican government had no policy of conferring refugee or asylum status. What Salvadorans were really looking for was physical security and economic opportunity—so they could take care of their families left behind. Many concluded that the best option was to go to the United States. Although they would not enjoy legal status, they could find personal safety and economic opportunities without going too far from home. What many found when they got to the U.S., however, was that U.S. immigration officials often denied them asylum, arguing that Salvadorans were economic migrants because they did not resettle in the countries closest to their homeland.

This discussion indicates how difficult it is to distinguish between the political and economic motives behind migration. Many Salvadorans were threatened with violence personally but, because they were important productive members of their families and lacked the resources necessary to leave, they did not flee immediately. Often, as in the cases of Santos and Jesús, people lived with the constant possibility of violent death and emigrated only when they were unable to meet the material needs of their families.

Traveling Mojado to the United States

If the foremost purpose of leaving El Salvador was to save their lives, Salvadorans who traveled to the United States overland encountered a multitude of new perils. Before the war began travel was not nearly as precarious. Salvadorans, particularly those from the middle and upper classes, could obtain tourist visas or even immigrant visas to enter the U.S. with relative ease. I interviewed a couple of the earliest Salvadoran migrants to Long Island who came in the prewar era. Don Miguel Yanes, one of these pioneers, was a civil servant from the small town of Concepción de Oriente in La Unión department. In 1971 a friend helped Don Miguel get a visa to the United States through government contacts and the two settled in New Cassel, Long Island (near Westbury). He found a job at a plastics factory. Eight years later he returned to his community of origin and told everyone about the opportunities on Long Island. This occurred just as the country headed into civil war. Within a short time after returning to the U.S., his townspeople, *Concepcioneros*, started showing up at his door asking for help to find housing and employment.

Miguel's compatriots were unable to obtain tourist visas and traveled to the U.S. as *mojados*, wetbacks or undocumented immigrants. Like Mexicans, Salvadorans use the term mojado to describe their trip, but they must cross three rivers while Mexicans need only cross the Rio Grande, the border between Mexico and the United States. Salvadorans cross one river to enter Guatemala, another between Guatemala and Mexico and the third is the Rio Grande. This theme of the three crossings and the added suffering Salvadorans undergo is reflected in a ballad and movie called "Tres Veces Mojado" or "Three Times a Wetback" which was very popular on Long Island in the early 1990s.

Salvadorans must travel a long distance to reach the U.S. border, go through several countries, and face serious dangers along the way. To help overcome these obstacles, most pay for assistance. Smugglers or *coyotes* are available virtually everywhere; for a hefty fee they advertise "guaranteed" passage into the United States. The prices for this service vary by comfort level. The highest prices are paid for coyotes (often operating through semi-legitimate travel agencies) to arrange counterfeit visitors' visas for their clients. In 1990 one of these visas cost around $5000, but that figure has surely increased since then. When undetected as fake, these visas allow individuals to fly directly into the United States or into Tijuana, Mexico where they cross the nearby border by land. There is always a risk that these visas will be detected as fake at the beginning or end of their journeys and immigrants generally get sent back home, losing their money. The cheaper alternative is to travel by bus under coyote escort. In 1990, this option was averaging $1800; informants told me that it had risen to $3000 by 1995. Typically, coyotes will gather a busload or more of clients and then set off up the ithsmus through Guatemala and Mexico. Coyotes develop relationships with these countries' officials, generally paying them bribes to allow their passengers through. However, there is truly no guarantee; in the 1990s passage through Mexico in particular has become much more precarious. Documentation exists of coyotes and officials robbing migrants, abusing them and then sending them back home (USCR 1991). If this happens, migrants lose their entire investment and have to start all over again. The cost of migrating is more than the typical Salvadoran would earn over several years. Consequently, most of the money is borrowed from relatives or friends living in the United States. Once migrants successfully cross the border into the U.S., they begin the painful process of finding enough income to pay off this major loan while sustaining themselves as well as their families in El Salvador. This is not easy; it is but the culmination of a long series of trials that Salvadorans endured during the war and on their journeys to the U.S.

The travails migrants face during the thousand mile or more journey to the United States are numerous and I cannot do justice to all of them here. They include long walks through deserts with little water or food, the constant threat of detection and deportation by government officials in the countries they pass through, the possibility of being strip searched by thieves, smugglers and officials who slit open the seams of travelers' clothing looking for hidden money, as well as drownings in the rivers, and separation and abandonment. Women are often the victims of rape and other forms of sexual abuse.

Carmen was detained by the Mexican authorities and kept in a shack. She told me about hiding behind a door while the Mexican police known as *federales* raped and beat several women who were caught with her. The trials and tribulations do not stop once people have passed over the border into the United States. Near San Diego, undocumented immigrants have been killed by speeding cars as they try to cross the highways; others have suffocated by hiding in airtight tractor trailers used to get them into the country.

Margarita recalls her near-death experience vividly. "There were 150 people in the trailer...and it was completely dark inside. There was only a very little window through which the air entered and we were nearly asphyxiated. Two children almost died. The coyotes left us inside the trailer outside a gas station for nearly a day. They left us theoretically to arrange our passage but they left all 150 of us inside, not knowing what they were doing....We didn't have anything inside all day—no water, no food. We hadn't eaten anything since we left Mexico. When they opened the trailer door we all fell out onto the ground gasping for breath.

Sonia's border story illustrates how the difficult journey also challenges their humanity. When Sonia was walking through the Arizona desert after crossing the border, her fellow mojados found two children huddled under a bush. They had been separated from their group and were lost. Sonia and several others tried to convince their coyote to take the children along, but he refused, saying they would slow the whole group down. Finally, one man, thinking of his own children, agreed to carry them.

Elements of danger and daring can be found in every immigrant's personal account of their journeys to the United States. Sister Maria's trip was not very eventful until she reached the Suichiate River which divides Guatemala and Mexico. She had taken a bus through Guatemala legally because Salvadorans do not need a visa for that country. But she did not have authorization to enter Mexico and had to enter by illegally crossing the river. "The only thing we had with us was a change of clothes, nothing more," she recounted. "One to wear to cross the river and the other to change into. But when we were crossing the river the thieves came out. They threw stones at us. They told us that if we didn't give them money they'd let the river carry us away. They were on horses and we were on foot. When they found anything on us they took it away. They searched us when we crossed the river and were putting on our shoes. They took everything and left us only with the clothes we had on....They took the money from the coyote first because they knew he was the one with the most money. But what I had done in El Salvador was to sew the money below the sleeves of my shirt. For as long as they searched me no money fell out, they didn't find anything. They searched me in my underwear, in my bra, everything. But they didn't find money. I was carrying one hundred dollars. One hundred dollars which my cousin gave me saying, 'Don't give these to anyone! Take these with you. They're going to help you.'"

With Maria's money the group continued on to Matamorros, Mexico. There, another coyote demanded an additional $500 to bring them across the border. The coyote threatened Maria if she delayed paying her: "She said to me, 'I can throw you out here in Texas. I can leave you here so that the Migra [INS] finds you. If you don't pay me the $500 I will leave you here....I will dump you wherever I want to.'" Maria made a desperate call to her relatives on Long Island and some days later she received the money to pay the coyote. The group then headed for the Rio Grande. "We crossed the river and had to cross running so that the Migra wouldn't catch us because there were helicopters all over....When a helicopter came by we would throw ourselves on the ground....We ran and hid from about nine o'clock to about two in the morning....The helicopters have a light but they didn't see us because when they came by we would hide in the bushes and when the helicopter had passed we would run to the other side. When the helicopter would return we'd run into the bushes again."

The group walked all night and Maria, who was several months pregnant, felt cramps but could not rest until they reached the safe house. There she remained for several days under watchful guard of the coyote until money from her relatives on Long Island was wired and she was released. While in Texas and before leaving for Long Island, Maria filed an application for political asylum with a local non-profit organization. In El Salvador, she had been a nun working with the poor in the countryside. She received many threats but ignored them until two men kidnapped and raped her, telling her she would be killed if she told anyone. Afterward, pregnant by her rapists and horrified of being attacked again, she fled the country without letting anyone know the reason, even her Mother Superior. She presented this information in Texas on her asylum application and was given permission by the INS to stay. Later, she was one of the few to win her case.

Maria was one of the lucky ones. About a third of those I interviewed were caught by the INS upon crossing the border. They describe being interrogated by officials and incarcerated in the INS detention centers known as *corralones*. During much of the 1980s, Salvadorans and other Central Americans were intimidated by the INS to give up their right to seek asylum and agree to leave the country "voluntarily." They were not regularly informed of their rights until a 1987 Supreme Court decision obligated the INS to provide this information to them. Some were also physically abused and conditions in the corralones are often deplorable.

After talking to Salvadorans about their trips, I always concluded our conversations by whether they would recommend that their friends or relatives come to the United States, knowing all that they had learned during their journeys and experiences. Nearly everyone answered the same way. They did not know that the trip would be so difficult; women particularly assert their desire never to repeat the experience. But they also find life in the United States more onerous than they expected. The reasons why they feel disappointed and somewhat disillusioned will be provided in the next two chapters. Over time the vision Salvadoran immigrants brought with them about what life would be like in the U.S. is distorted by their real-life experiences here. They often become disillusioned, like Roberto. "I would tell them not to come," he insisted. "The only thing that we do here is suffer....First you leave your family, your wife, your children. Sometimes there isn't any work here. Sometimes you are sick and you still have to work. Here if you don't have work you can't survive. If you don't have money to pay the rent or buy food, you die of hunger."

3

Employment and Economic Symbiosis

It is late May on Long Island and by 6:00 AM the nighttime hibernation has given way to a flurry of activity. Legions of sleepy commuters cradle mugs of coffee as they roll up their garage doors and slip behind the wheel. Minutes later they cruise onto smaller and then larger thoroughfares that clog with similar sojourners headed for offices on Long Island and in New York City some thirty to fifty miles away. From their air-conditioned and stereophonic berths they may observe a parallel yet distinct awakening. Landscapers' trucks lumber by, hauling trailers full of lawn mowers, hedge cutters and leaf blowers. The trucks stop momentarily, only the few seconds needed for men in tee-shirts, jeans, work boots and baseball caps to jump aboard. Less than two months into the landscaping season these Salvadoran laborers are baked deep brown by the sun and the soil has implanted itself firmly beneath their fingernails. They will toil from dawn to dusk manicuring Long Islanders' properties, but as these groups' paths cross again in the evening, the commuters see only sweaty, stained foreigners trodding the groomed streets of their village.

In the early morning sunlight, immigrant women in freshly starched uniforms and pinafores walk briskly from their apartments downtown to the spacious homes where they labor as maids and nannies. Speeding by them on bicycles are compatriots who are returning home after working the graveyard shift at nearby factories. A stone's throw away, dozens of men are congregating in front of a local deli where they hope that someone will offer them a day's work painting, mowing, or cleaning. As local contractors stop in front, these men swarm around the vehicle hoping to be selected and not go home to a mattress on the floor and empty pockets, like they did yesterday. As the day laborers wait, cars full of other Salvadorans race by, their occupants en route to factories and fast-food restaurants. For $10 to $20 a week, a friend or co-worker provides transportation to and from work—a godsend because the public transportation system on Long Island is notoriously poor.

For months I observed this daily spectacle each morning in Goldcoast. It became quite clear that there were many job opportunities on the island for immigrants and that these people were not moving to the island after a rite of passage in the inner city. This pattern runs counter to well-known theories of immigrant settlement which hold that immigrants first enter the cities and then move to the suburbs as they become successful. And one might suppose that Salvadorans would find more job opportunities and acceptance in the inner city. Elsewhere in the United States, Salvadorans do conform to these theories, settling in cities such as Los Angeles, San Francisco, Houston, and Washington, D.C. and also in parts of New York City such as Jamaica and Flushing, Queens. However, Salvadorans on Long Island by and large migrate directly there from their homeland, spending little if any time in cities. Why?

Why, moreover, are Salvadorans moving to Long Island at a time when many native Long Islanders, especially young workers and their families are leaving because of expensive housing and the high cost of living? On the face of it, these factors should discourage poor immigrant workers from settling as well. Finally, why are Salvadoran workers found in very narrow sectors of the Long Island employment spectrum? Almost all are blue-collar workers; very few have been able to obtain pink-collar office positions or have professional occupations. The main areas of Salvadoran employment on the island are in the service sector and, to a lesser degree, manufacturing. The reasons for why they have limited occupational opportunities are varied but fall into two general categories: characteristics of the immigrants themselves and characteristics of the Long Island economy where they find jobs.

PROFILE OF SALVADORAN WORKERS ON LONG ISLAND

Salvadorans form a labor force with specific characteristics and obligations that leave them little alternative but to work for low wages and accept poor working conditions. They are frequently exploited. For most Salvadorans, particularly those from rural backgrounds, this status is still an improvement over their status in El Salvador where they also occupied the bottom of the job hierarchy yet often could not support their families adequately.

The most important social characteristics that have limited Salvadorans' job opportunities have been their legal status and their low levels of education and marketable skills. Until 1991 when Salvadorans were finally offered Temporary Protected Status (TPS) by the federal government after a decade of litigation, the vast majority were undocumented. Until 1988 when employer sanctions under IRCA went into effect, undocumented Salvadorans found work relatively easily because the demand for labor was high. After sanctions went into effect, certain employers became more careful about checking their employees' work authorization because they feared being fined by the government. This was more true of factory owners and fast-food chains and less true of people who employed immigrants as nannies and landscapers.

Salvadorans' job prospects are also limited by their low levels of formal education and limited English-language ability. Adult Salvadorans I surveyed averaged 6.4 years of education and fully a third had achieved less than five years of schooling. The vast majority of the Long Island Salvadoran population speaks English poorly. This proportion may be dropping as large numbers of immigrants attend English classes and learn the language in their workplace, but I have been told repeatedly by close informants that English is their greatest obstacle to socioeconomic mobility. Few of the skills Salvadorans bring with them are applicable to the lives they lead in suburbia. Many knew how to farm but this knowledge has been of little use to them here. "When I first got here, everything was very hard for me," Santos recalled. As a peasant in Morazán department, he had sowed his own crops and harvested coffee before he emigrated. "Everything, everything that I knew how to do was useless to me here—how to work the land, harvest corn, plant beans and so on. Here these skills were of no use to me at all." After several months of unemployment, Santos found work cleaning a factory by night and later as a landscaper. Some Salvadoran men claim they have an affinity for landscaping because they work outside with nature much like they did in their homeland. Other immigrants, particularly South Americans from middle-class backgrounds, despise this work as too humble and are happy to leave it to the *guanacos* [Salvadorans] (Mahler 1992).

PROFILE OF SALVADORANS' EMPLOYMENT OPPORTUNITIES

Salvadorans are found in several sectors of the Long Island economy. One main area of employment is providing services to Long Island households. Men and women both work in this sector, but their jobs are gender specific. Men work outside as landscapers, construction workers, pool maintenance laborers, and grave diggers. Salvadoran women generally work inside, serving as *internas* or live-in maids, house cleaners, and nannies. They also work in restaurants, and cater parties and provide care to the elderly. During a typical work week, women often perform several of these activities. Sonia, a Salvadoran woman in her late thirties, divides her time between McDonalds and housecleaning. Early in the morning, she walks a mile to the fast food restaurant. She flips hamburgers until five and returns home to where her children, five, seven and thirteen, have been watching T.V. since the end of school. When she is not at McDonalds on Tuesdays and Sundays, she cleans several houses for extra cash. Her McDonalds job pays only minimum wage, about

$5,000 per year, and Sonia cannot support her family on those wages, despite sharing an apartment with her brother. Her husband lives separately and provides child support very sporadically—usually when Sonia's daughter throws a tantrum, begging for a new dress or pair of shoes. He is a landscaper and, like most landscapers, his work is seasonal. Landscapers are employed almost exclusively by second-generation Italian immigrants whose parents once labored in the jobs Salvadorans hold today (LaGumina 1988). Landscapers suffer a period of high unemployment every year from December into March. This affects women as well as men since many Long Islanders spend the winter in the south and do not need house cleaning and other services during this time. Salvadorans often comment that women find work easier than men; however, this has not led men to invade traditionally female jobs.

Many Salvadorans are employed in consumer services such as restaurants (both fast-food and ethnic establishments), office cleaning, car care, and in large retail stores. Their positions are directly related to their degree of English fluency. In fast-food restaurants such as McDonalds and even the California Pizza Factory, Salvadorans are concentrated in food preparation and clean-up while native workers take orders and serve as cashiers. The lines are less rigid in ethnic usually Italian—restaurants but there is still a built-in pecking order. New hires invariably begin as dishwashers. Over time they are shifted to busboys, assistant cooks, and finally cooks. The dishwasher's knowledge that he will earn a good salary as a cook in several years' time rarely appeases him because he is performing a female job. "The guy, who was a peasant in El Salvador and becomes a dishwasher here, feels bad," Don José told me. "He washes dishes but it's a women's job. For him only women should wash dishes and sometimes he doesn't want to say what he does. He feels bad, he feels humiliated when he gets a job washing dishes." Commercial and industrial cleaning is also humbling for Salvadoran men who often toil alongside women. But this work carries the advantage of being performed largely a night when it is less likely to catch the attention of the INS.

Another major area of Salvadoran employment is manufacturing. For decades, Long Island's industrial base was dominated by defense manufacturers whose labor force was well-paid and highly unionized. This high-wage end of the spectrum in not populated by Salvadorans, who have found employment in smaller industries—sometimes those which supply the giant defense companies—which produce plastics, metals, condiments, cosmetics, direct mailings and other items. Many Salvadorans also make a living or supplement their salaries by providing services and products to their co-ethnics. These activities range from formal businesses such as Salvadoran restaurants and remittance agencies to informal endeavors such as babysitting and making Salvadoran specialties like *pupusas* (cheese or meat filled corn tortillas) and *tamales* (cornmeal with chicken or pork and other seasonings rolled into banana leaves) at home.

The village of Hempstead in central Nassau County has become the Salvadoran nexus on the island. It is home to some 3,500 Salvadorans, according to the 1990 census as well as more than a dozen Salvadoran and other Latino eateries, numerous remittance, travel, employment and insurance agencies (what I refer to as "multiservice" agencies), a couple of Spanish-language newspapers, and several social service agencies that cater specifically to the Salvadorans. In September, Hempstead is also the site of the island's Central American Independence Day parade, an event which draws thousands of Salvadorans and other immigrants to proudly celebrate their heritage. Suffolk County's counterpart to Hempstead is Brentwood. Long an area of Puerto Rican settlement, Brentwood has taken on a distinctive Salvadoran flavor in recent years. Soccer teams compete on the municipal fields, and the main streets house numerous Salvadoran restaurants, multiservice agencies, and even a lawyer's office.

The cluster of Latino-owned businesses in these two towns is striking but should not be confused with an ethnic enclave. An enclave is a place largely separate from the greater economy where large numbers of an ethnic group find employment in businesses owned by co-ethnics (Portes and Back 1985; Zhou 1992). Enclaves offer newcomers an option to low-wage, low-status jobs in the larger economy. Immigrants can work with their compatriots and use their own language. On Long Island there are dozens of Latino-owned businesses, but even in Hempstead and Brentwood they do not constitute an enclave. This is because they do not employ at least a third of Salvadoran workers in the area. Rather, they are small in size, employ few workers, and, to my knowledge, there are no manufacturers owned by Salvadorans. The ethnic sector makes a stronger visual than economic impact. Still, it does fill an important niche left vacant by the larger society—services aimed specifically at an immigrant and Spanish-speaking public—and Salvadorans regularly travel to Hempstead and Brentwood from other parts of the island to frequent these businesses.

Perhaps more Salvadorans earn a living by performing informal services to other immigrants than by working in the formal ethnic sector. The "informal economy" has been defined as *"all income-earning activities that are not regulated by the state in social environments where similar activities are regulated"* (Castells and Portes 1989:12, emphasis in the original). In other words, people who work within the informal economy are paid off the books and are a kind of workforce in the shadows. On Long Island, immigrants have developed a variety of informal entrepreneurial activities. For example, many women with young children cannot work outside the home because child care is too expensive. Sometimes they turn their homes into informal day care centers for friends' and relatives' children, usually charging $50 a week for the service—one third or less than typical fees; other times they cook for their housemates.

Noemí Orellana awakens before sunrise each morning to prepare lunches for several landscape laborers who live in the house she rents. They pay her $50 per week for meals and she nets $400 a month, barely enough for Noemí to support herself and her daughter. When time permits, Noemí also sells Mary Kay cosmetics to other Salvadoran women in her neighborhood. When Amalia Sandoval's son was born in 1990 with a heart defect, she could no longer work cleaning rooms at the hotel where she had been employed. With the help of her friends, Amalia began sewing Salvadoran-style clothes for sale, party dresses in particular. She had been a seamstress in her home town in El Salvador and the skill came in handy on Long Island where it was difficult to find this style—satiny pastel-colored dresses that billow out from the waist—in the stores. Originally, her clientele did not extend beyond the large apartment complex where Amalia lived, but after a few of her dresses had been debuted around town at dances and weddings, she had difficulty filling all her orders on time.

Men are also involved in informal activities. I estimate that around two dozen men who enjoy legal status have begun working as informal personal couriers, traveling back and forth between the United States and El Salvador bringing letters, packages, and remittances. Known as *viajeros*, they customize their service to certain towns on Long Island and in El Salvador, usually traveling between their town of origin and their town or resettlement. Sonia's uncle has been earning a living this way for four years. He operates out of his sister's apartment; a few days before he leaves for El Salvador, streams of clients come by to give him their goods to send home; meanwhile his sister cooks tamales to sell to his clients as well. Since she normally stays home every day with her young son, this is her only opportunity to earn spending money.

A discussion of the Long Island employment structure for Salvadorans would not be complete without referring to the prevailing wages immigrants receive. According to the survey I conducted in 1989-90, the median weekly salary for Salvadorans is $229 (or $12,000 per year). This income level is far lower than the $450.47 weekly average for all Long Island workers (NYS Business Statistics Quarterly Summary 1989). Hourly wages vary from job to job but generally range between $5 and $7. According to my survey, the median hourly wage of immigrant kitchen helpers, construction workers and commercial cleaners was around $5. Factory workers (operators) earned slightly less at $4.50 and cooks' helpers slightly more at $5.50. The highest median wage was paid to landscapers who earned $6.25 per hour. Keep in mind that these figures are median values and there is a range of salaries. Live-in maids earn between $150 and $200 per week for six days of work. Though internas are given room and board and therefore have few costs, the job's meager pay and social isolation contribute to its low desirability.

"You save a lot of money this way, working live-in," explains Altagracia Sánchez. "But there are many women who don't like this because they get bored. It's not easy spending your life slaving to the wishes of your boss." Like many other young Salvadoran women, Altagracia worked as an interna taking care of an elderly woman shortly after arriving in the U.S. As soon as she could, she found work cleaning houses. Such work is better paid; house cleaners typically earn $8 to $10 per hour in cash, although it is not easy to find enough houses to clean to keep busy all week. Altagracia currently cleans only three houses one week and four the next. The $150 to $200 is not enough to care adequately for herself and her five year-old son. To economize, they sleep in the living room of a small apartment while another couple occupies the lone bedroom.

House cleaners frequently complain that there are too many women seeking jobs and that they have flooded the market, even lowering their hourly rate to win contracts from other Salvadorans. House cleaning can also be dangerous because many Salvadoran women are unfamiliar with cleaning products used in the U.S. and cannot read the labels in order to protect themselves properly. "I once touched Easy-Off cleaner with my hands and I burned my fingers," Luz Aguilar explained. She is from the capital city of San Salvador and had received a university education before she emigrated, but she still did not know enough English to prepare herself. "It happened because I wasn't familiar with this product and I couldn't read the label and my boss didn't tell me that I should use gloves with it. Another thing is ammonia. The label says that you have to dilute it with water but I used it plain and it made me cry. I couldn't even breathe from the strength of the smell. And that was because I didn't know English and I didn't know how to read the labels." Working with noxious and often toxic substances and the sheer physical strenuousness of the job are the principal reasons women leave house cleaning, particularly when they become pregnant. They sacrifice the relatively high pay and flexibility of house cleaning for factory jobs which offer benefits such as health insurance, or for jobs in the informal sector which allow the women to stay at home yet derive some income.

Suburban Symbiosis

The types of jobs and level of income that Salvadorans obtain on Long Island place them squarely within the ranks of the working poor. This position is reinforced by the high cost of living on the island (Yago et al. 1987). Given these facts, why are Salvadorans be attracted to Long Island over other areas where at least living costs are less expensive? A few Salvadorans told me that they were enticed to Long Island by promises of wages which averaged fifty cents higher than wages in other parts of the country. Only upon arrival did they find out that their costs of living—specifically those associated with the winter season such as heating oil and heavy clothing—would also be higher and compensate for the increased wages. But the story behind the Long Island magnet is much more complicated than this and requires a closer look at Long Island's history and economic development.

Long Island: A Brief Historical Sketch

At the turn of the twentieth century Long Island was a sparsely populated area devoted to farming potatoes and onions; there were few, if any, clues that the countryside would become home to dozens of housing developments and two and a half million people. The World War II period witnessed especially dramatic transformations as the island was massively suburbanized and its economy and population grew. By the 1980s and 1990s, the "baby boom" children had grown up. Real estate prices had risen so much that few could stay in the communities they grew up in. They moved away from the island or out to eastern Suffolk county, leaving their parents behind. These demographic shifts opened up opportunities in the low-pay, low-skill end of the labor market because there were few young workers to take them and more senior citizens who needed inexpensive services.

The new niches provided employment opportunities for Salvadorans and other immigrants.

In the early part of this century the North Shore area of Long Island was known as the "Gold Coast," playground of the super rich (Smits 1974). All along the coast the wealthiest New York families, such as the Woolworths, Pratts, Graces and Morgans, built summer mansions. Many earlier immigrants were brought to the island to staff these estates. Southern Italian villagers served as gardeners (LaGumina 1988) and many of the laundresses, nannies, and housekeepers were Scottish, Irish, African-American and Italian. In fact, though Long Island is often stereotyped as racially and ethnically homogenous, in reality it has a legacy of diversity and immigration (LaGumina 1988; 1980).

In the first decades of the twentieth century, aviation became an increasingly integral part of the Nassau County economy, Roosevelt Field at its heart. Originally used by the military during World Wars I and II, the prime real estate in the center of the county was later subdivided into tracts for housing and a shopping mall which now bears the field's name. But the key importance of Roosevelt airfield was that it helped spawn the development of many major defense industries on Long Island, including the Sperry Aircraft Company and Grumman (Smits 1974). During World War II the defense/aerospace industry thrived and expanded, becoming the anchor of the island's economy.

Following World War II, Long Island was dramatically transformed into quintessential suburbia. The land was altered into the vision of what middle America should be: single-family homes with a yard, two parents and several children. The demand for this lifestyle did not stem from a desire to return to prewar normalcy few could afford economically-independent nuclear families during the Depression and the war). Nor was the demand fueled only by the critical housing shortage which emerged as GIs returned home (by 1947, six million families in the U.S. were living doubled-up with relatives or friends [Jackson 1985:232]). Rather, developers turned the housing shortage into a postwar building boom that patterned the landscape and also structured family and neighborhood life (ibid.). Perhaps most notorious of the developers were the Levitts, who perfected mass production techniques as they built entire planned communities in the heart of Long Island. Federal loans enabled veterans to buy new houses with very small down payments. When Abraham Levitt announced the sale of 350 homes at a cost of $7,990—$90 down and $58 a month mortgage payments to begin on Monday March 7, 1949—people began forming a line on the preceding Friday. In the next two and a half years the Levitts would build 17,500 homes in the area.

Economic Development on the Island

As hundreds of thousands of urbanites were drawn to the Long Island suburbs by the promise of inexpensive housing they formed a large labor pool. In the early phases of this suburbanization, most new Long Island workers commuted back to work in New York City. As the years passed, the local economy expanded and absorbed most of the Long Island labor force. Only one-third of Nassau county's workers and one-seventh of Suffolk county's still commute to New York City, this group occupies a disproportionate number of the highest-paid jobs in the city (Yago et al. 1987:11).

Economic development on Long Island was originally anchored by the defense industry; later it expanded into other manufacturing areas as well as into many types of services. Beginning with the founding of several aircraft and aerospace companies early in the century (Smits 1974; Thruelson 1976), the defense industry was nurtured by World War II, the Cold War, space exploration in the 1970s, and the military buildup of the 1980s. Long Island's economy became "constructed around a core of Grumman and four other major government contractors (Allied-Signal, Unisys, Harris, and Lockheed) which specialized in technologically sophisticated aerospace weaponry" (Carmean et al. n.d.:7). These "core" defense industries fostered the growth a much more extensive array of "peripheral," dependent firms supplying manufactured goods and specialty services, such as accounting, management consultants and lobbyists, to the core industries (ibid:11). Until the downscaling of the U.S. military in the

1990s, the Big Five Contractors and their trading network dominated the local economy, accounting for some 72 percent of the industrial jobs in the region (ibid.:8). The cutbacks in federal spending on military contracts during the 1990s has had severe repercussions on the island's defense industry, but during the 1980s—the years of greatest Salvadoran immigration—the Reagan administration increased military spending and buoyed the Long Island defense establishment. The spoils were enjoyed by the Salvadorans and other immigrant workers as well, because they labored for firms that subcontracted to the big defense companies.

Salvadoran manufacturing workers are not employed by the large, "core" industries; rather, many obtain jobs in firms which supply plastic and metal parts to the giant firms. The smaller companies compete among themselves for contracts from the core firms. Consequently, they pay wages of some $4 to $6 per hour (and generally without benefits), much lower than the salaries of workers, managers, and engineers in the core industries. Needless to say, the small companies suffer from the boom and bust cycles of major defense contractors. The combination of low pay, lack of benefits and likelihood of layoffs is unattractive to native-born workers who need to earn a salary sufficient to raise a family in an expensive area of the country. This has created an opening for immigrant and particularly undocumented immigrant workers who tend to be more pliable workers.

In addition to the defense-related contractors, immigrants work in other light industries on Long Island which manufacture products like cabinets, furniture, plastic household goods, condiments, cosmetics, spare car parts, and grocery carts to name a few. Salvadorans entered this sector of the Long Island economy in large numbers after they acquired temporary legal status in the early 1990s. Before that time, these companies, vulnerable to raids by immigration authorities because they hire many workers, tended to check work authorization more rigorously than employers in the service sectors of the economy. Unfortunately, Salvadorans' foothold in Long Island manufacturing may be short-lived. When President Clinton decided not to renew this temporary status in December 1994, only extending their work authorization another nine months to September 1995 (later extended through January 1996), many Salvadorans were fired from their jobs in January 1995 by employers who feared sanctions and misunderstood the president's directive.

If manufacturing expanded on Long Island in the 1980s, other sectors of the economy have grown even more rapidly and absorbed more of the local labor force. These sectors include trade, finance, insurance and real estate (FIRE) and services. Wholesale and retail trade accounted for twice as many jobs as manufacturing on Long Island in 1989, as did the service sector (New York State Department of Labor 1990). Employment by local and regional governments alone employed more individuals than did manufacturing while the FIRE sector employed half as many. These sectors of the economy employed very few Salvadorans, however. Although some Salvadorans found work in restaurants and a few in retail stores, hardly any work in health care, education, and social services where knowledge of English is a necessity. The growth in these other areas of the economy affected Salvadorans indirectly: by providing opportunities for the native-born labor force, vacancies were created at the low-end of the labor market, a niche perfect for the immigrants.

To summarize, Long Island's economy over the past decades was marked by a massive expansion. Perhaps the most striking difference between Long Island and its metropolitan neighbor, New York City, is the fact that Long Island's manufacturing industries have largely avoided the phenomenon of deindustrialization, the "widespread systematic disinvestment in the nation's basic productive capacity" (Bluestone & Harrison 1982:6). They have suffered from military cutbacks but this has been compensated for by the area's transformation into a post-industrial economy, one characterized by a high reliance on service industries.

Demographic Changes Affect the Work Force

Post World War II Long Island has also been marked by major demographic changes which have played an important role in opening job opportunities for Salvadorans. The rising demand for domestic workers is a good example. It is the product of three inter-related characteristics of the Long Island work force: the incorporation of more women into the labor force; the affluence of an echelon of Long Island families, particularly dual-income households and households with commuters into New York City, and growth of the senior citizen population. Throughout the United States, the ideal of a stay-at-home mother became imperiled in the 1970s as the buying power of household incomes stagnated and declined. This trend continued through the 1980s as women's labor force participation on Long Island "rose from 50.1 percent in 1980 to 56.7 percent in 1988" (NYS DOL 1990:57). Women's entry created a demand for domestic services such as childcare and housecleaning, mainly performed by women. I label this the "Zoë Baird phenomenon," named after the corporate attorney who was nominated by President Clinton in early 1993 to become U.S. Attorney General. She later removed her name from consideration when it was revealed that she had knowingly hired undocumented domestic workers (in defiance of immigration law) and had failed to pay Social Security taxes on their earnings, also required by law. The disclosure of Baird's gaffe as well as similar incidents with other prominent officials—even California's governor Pete Wilson who has been a leader in the anti-immigrant movement of the 1990s—have sent shudders throughout Long Island where similar employment practices are ubiquitous (*Newsday*, February 10, 1993). As more women entered the work force, there was also a growing demand for workers to perform traditional male jobs such as lawn cutting and house painting. By hiring immigrants to perform these services at reasonable costs middle- and upper-class families could enjoy both a higher standard of living and some leisure time.

Other major demographic changes afoot on Long Island also created demand for immigrant services. The most dramatic were the precipitous decline in the local birthrate and the gradual graying of the population. Long Island had been one of the epicenters of the baby boom of the 1950s but there was a baby bust by the late 1960s. This drop in the birth rate affected the local supply of young workers, people available for low-wage jobs in particular. Specifically, the number of young workers (ages 15 to 24) fell by nearly 100,000 between 1980 and 1990. Astronomic increases in the cost of housing and maintaining a family on Long Island in the 1980s also are responsible for driving young Long Islanders away. For instance, the average selling price for homes on Long Island tripled from $78,290 in 1982 to $224,098 in 1988 (Long Island Almanac 1989). Clearly, the escalating cost of housing has become a disincentive to staying in the region to such an extent that "the area's economic growth is being negatively affected by the shortage of affordable housing" (NYS DOL:1988:15).

In contrast to the youthful Long Islanders, the senior citizen population rose in the past decades, from 7.8 percent in 1970 to 12.4 percent in 1990. This trend is expected to accelerate during the 1990s and beyond. Many of today's seniors purchased their homes at low prices after World War II and watched the value of their real estate skyrocket in the 1980s. This was a mixed blessing; the value of their homes increased but they had to pay higher real estate taxes and often could not sell their properties because few buyers could afford them. The result has been that many older Long Islanders have stayed put even after their children have moved away. Some have rented their homes when they could not sell them.

The dual demographic shifts on Long Island have had significant ramifications for the local labor force. The decline in the native-born teenager and young worker population has placed these workers in a privileged position. They can command the best jobs within the low-paying sector, leaving the least desirable jobs to immigrants. The growth in the senior population has also spurred demand for low-cost labor, both for traditional services such as landscaping and house cleaning and also for growth industries in elder care. Older Long Islanders on fixed incomes and saddled with high real estate and school taxes are particularly concerned about hiring low-cost labor for these positions. Immigrant, particularly Salvadoran, labor has been critical in these areas.

Filling a Niche

Long Island's economy expanded and was robust throughout the 1980s but the available labor force was aging and shrinking. By the mid 1980s, official estimates put the labor force deficit at some thirty thousand workers per year (NYS DOL , personal communication). At the same time, the island supported a thriving informal economy suggesting that thousands more workers were needed than officially recorded. The demand was filled to some degree by New York City residents who began commuting to the island (e.g., *New York Daily News* November 10, 1989; *Newsday* November 22, 1989). Immigrants migrating directly to the island also constituted a dynamic new low-wage supply of labor.

Viewed in terms of the needs of the Long Islanders, as well as the immigrants, the relationship between these groups appears to be mutually beneficial. Salvadorans have benefited because they have found safe refuge from the civil war in their country and, for the most part, they have been able to support themselves and their families left behind. Long Islanders get cheap labor. "The gringo is not going to work for [the low salary the Hispanic makes]," Don José insisted. "He'll work for $10 an hour and only eight hours. If he wants to work more he'll work more but if he doesn't he won't. If he works more, he has to be paid overtime. The poor Hispanics work no matter what. In construction and in landscaping you only find Hispanics. Why? Because they're working like beasts of burden and the bosses pay them what they want." If there were no immigrants to take these types of jobs then employers would have to raise wages to attract native workers. This might drive the price of certain services such as lawn cutting and elder care too high for Long Island families to afford. Their standard of living would be affected.

Moreover, there is profit to be made by hiring immigrant workers. Employers save money by hiring immigrants off the books. It is the bosses not the employees who control the decision over who will be paid on and off the books and it is mostly to the bosses' advantage. By paying workers off the books, employers avoid paying Social Security, disability and unemployment taxes as well as benefits such as sick and va-

cation pay. Such outlays amount to a quarter or more of a typical salary; their nonpayment enhances employers' profit
margins.

HOW WORKERS FIND JOBS

Even when there is a ready demand for labor, it is not always
easy for Salvadorans to find the available jobs. Salvadorans
on Long Island rarely look for jobs by sending out resumes
or responding to newspaper advertisements. Rather, they
search for information through networks of family or
friends. Alonso Quintanilla is a manager at an industrial
laundry where all hiring is conducted this way. Alonso fled
El Salvador with his two young sons in early 1984 after a
close friend was murdered by a death squad. He moved to
the South Shore of Long Island where he had distant family
living and found work at the laundry. At first, his job en-
tailed mixing vats of the filthy hospital sheets soaked in
cleaning chemicals. Sometimes he had to handle the soiled
materials with his hands and the bleach would burn his
arms. Later the laundry was mechanized, but the workers
who do the dirtiest work sorting soiled sheets and towels are
all Salvadoran. They wear masks over their faces and gloves
on their hands; working in tandem they toss the laundry into
different bins which are then whisked away to huge washing
machines tended by other Salvadorans. Salvadorans catch
the clean laundry at the other end of the machine and steer
the bins to huge dryers and then on to lines of women who
pin the sheets and towels onto huge ironing drums. Another
cadre of women grab the wrinkleless sheets, already shrink-
wrapped in packages, and stack them onto new carts. These
carts are then piloted to waiting delivery trucks where fleets
of African-American men drive them to their destinations.

Alonso laughs when asked whether U.S. workers labored
with him. "You have got to be kidding. Whenever a gringo
starts working here he never lasts more than two days. People with documents would never put up with the conditions
that we [undocumented immigrants] have to. Sometimes
blacks would show up to work but they would get one whiff
of the horrible smell and the next thing you knew, they would

be gone." The Mexican plant manager readily admits that an informal recruitment system operates at laundry. Eighty percent of the employees are Salvadorans who are recruited through ethnic networks, through word of mouth recommendations from current employees. Turnover is a mere three percent and dozens of applicants arrive knocking on the door daily.

Aside from networks, some Salvadorans find jobs through job agencies and day labor shape-up points. Hempstead is home to three job agencies, all of which have reputations for taking fees and providing little assistance. They are another example of how certain enterprising individuals have found ways to profit from others' destitution. Salvadorans with no permanent job often gravitate to Long Island's shape-up points. According to Omar Henriquez of the Workplace Project, a center for workers' rights, there are currently seven such places where day laborers congregate on Long Island. The largest is in Franklin Square where at sunrise on any given day dozens of workers brave the heat or the cold, waiting for one day's work and the hope of earning $50. On average only 15 will be lucky. Sometimes contacts developed on the job will blossom into full-time work. More often, workers flock to the shape-up when they are in-between jobs or when the economy is particularly bad.

COPING WITH MISTREATMENT AND LOW WAGES

Despite the availability of work, and the obvious need for their services, low wages, exploitation and sudden layoffs often plague Salvadoran workers. One day when I was working in a social service agency, a 21 year-old Salvadoran came in. He was cradling an arm which was heavily bandaged and when I inquired about what had happened, he told me that he had been scalded when a pot of boiling water fell on his arm at his restaurant job. Despite pleading with his boss, he was not allowed to seek medical treatment until his shift ended. By that time the arm had swollen considerably and required several weeks of treatment and months of therapy. The employer refused to pay for the medical expenses and fired the Salvadoran when he could no longer perform his job with his bandaged arm. This case is not unusual. Immigrants tend to work in factories with machinery and in other high-risk occupations such as landscaping where accidents happen frequently. The Worplace Project was founded in Hempstead in 1994 to advocate on behalf of immigrants in cases such as this one, but they are too understaffed to handle all the requests for their services.

As an immigrant counselor, Elena has heard many stories about the abuse of her fellow Salvadorans. Now in her thirties, Elena was an organizer for a Catholic organization in the capital of El Salvador before she came to the United States. She was forced to flee the country when the government labeled her work with the poor as "subversive." When I asked her what challenges Salvadorans face in the job market, she responded, "You have problems if you don't have documents here. It has gotten more and more and more difficult to find decent work [since IRCA]. The next problem is the language. If you don't speak any English it is very difficult to find a job which pays you a decent wage. There are a lot of cases of exploitation; people who work in restaurants sometimes find themselves unpaid after two to three weeks and then they are fired. This also happens with people hired to clean buildings and they also are not paid....Only this past Sunday I was talking to a man who worked in a restaurant and he hadn't been paid for the last two weeks he worked there. They still haven't paid him. And since employers often pay workers in cash there is no way to prove they haven't been paid."

The obstacles Salvadorans face might seem insurmountable to many Americans, but immigrants cannot afford the luxury of rejecting undesirable jobs. They not only need an income to support themselves but also to support the people depending upon them back home. And, to repeat, undocumented immigrants and even Salvadorans with TPS/DED status do not qualify for public benefits except Medicaid for emergency and prenatal care. Therefore, they have no government safety net to fall back on if they cannot support themselves. For Salvadorans it is imperative that they find and keep a job. This is especially critical, but most difficult, just after arrival in the U.S. when they are saddled with an enormous travel debt and know little about where to find work. Immigrants feel compelled to take any job they can find, regardless of the working conditions, and they will do most anything to keep it. This makes them very dependable workers, a quality esteemed by their employers, but also makes them vulnerable to exploitation.

Salvadorans are willing to accept jobs that offer low wages and little prestige at least in part because they measure wages and prestige on a different scale than Americans do. To Salvadorans, $5 per hour is a wage superior to what they would be earning in their homeland and the money that they are able to send to their families there goes much further in El Salvador than it would in the U.S. Thus, when they measure their pre-migration status against their current status, they feel that they have accomplished something and their stature is elevated. This immigrant perspective fades for the children of immigrants, the second generation. Unlike their parents, the members of the second generation see themselves primarily within the U.S. hierarchy and measure themselves accordingly. They tend to be much less satisfied with their social position than their parents (Suárez-Orozco 1989).

Salvadorans have innovated ways to compensate for their low wages. Unlike many native-born Long Islanders, immigrants can survive on a sub-family wage. The strategies they use are diverse, beginning with living extremely austere lives. Most live in densely populated and substandard housing. Several places I entered stand out in my memory. One was an apartment of an undocumented Salvadoran and her family in Goldcoast. When I entered through the back door it took a minute for my eyes to adjust to the darkness, despite being midday. As I stepped inside, the floor creaked ominously and I felt like my feet would fall through. Roaches skittered on a table laden with containers of food and boxes of laundry detergent. The ceiling had collapsed over the hallway and that there was a persistent drip from the bathroom. When I asked to look further, I saw water dripping from the ceiling, leaving wet plaster smeared all over the shower floor. My hostess, suckling her younger child to her breast, explained that every time her upstairs neighbors used the shower the water rained down into her bathroom, rendering it useless. The landlord refused her appeals to make repairs despite the $1150 she paid in rent. In order to afford this high rent, six adults and two children—all members of an extended family—shared space in the two bedrooms.

Many Salvadorans also compensate for their low salaries by maintaining their families in El Salvador where children are much less expensive to raise. Sometimes children born in the U.S. are also sent back, at least until they are of school age. Salvadorans also economize by minimizing their personal expenditures. When this is not enough, they increase the hours at their jobs or find additional employment. Salvadorans have also created institutions paralleling those of the mainstream society in which a small group of entrepreneurs have profited. They earn what I call "surplus income" by using their private cars as pseudo-taxis, charging other immigrants fees to drive them to work and the grocery store. Salvadorans have also devised housing system whereby the leaseholder of a rented apartment or house sublets space within the unit to many individuals. As I explain in the next chapter, leaseholders, or *encargados*, obtain enough income from their boarders that they themselves live on the properties for free and may even earn a profit.

Longitudinal Changes in Salvadorans Employment

Follow-up fieldwork and interviews I conducted in 1994-5, five years after my initial research, offer little evidence of significant occupational or socioeconomic mobility, even among those enjoying legal status. Most key informants were still performing the same jobs they had in 1990 and had received only modest salary increases. Edgar, for example, still works in pool maintenance for the same company. He earns a few dollars more per hour than when he started, but he is still unemployed for several months during the off-season. His wife, Yolanda, was able to leave the live-in maid position she found shortly after arriving in the U.S. in 1988, but despite the secretarial credentials she earned in El Salvador, she works primarily cleaning houses and babysitting. Recently, the family that used to hire her as a maid, offered her two days of office work but only because they know her personally. (They are also still sponsoring her for her green card.) She is studying for her high school equivalency exam (GED) but knows that a real office job is many years away. Roberto has also experienced little job advancement over the years. He worked for the same landscaping company without a raise for four years. He finally was offered another position pruning trees for a dollar more per hour. Roberto supplements this job driving for a fellow immigrant who sells jewelry door-to-door. Despite six to seven days of work, he still lives in a tiny room which he shares with a nephew.

Although they have experienced only extremely limited employment gains, the money Salvadorans send back home has often improved the socioeconomic status of their family there. Edgar, for instance, is building a $40,000 home for his uncle, brothers and other relatives in the San Vicente department of El Salvador. The large concrete structure with a wide veranda is replacing the one room shack in which Edgar grew up. Similarly, Roberto has just financed the immigration of his sister for $3,000 and has also supported his large family who live in La Libertad department.

There are a few cases of Salvadorans I know who were educated in their homeland and, after starting at the bottom and learning English, have acquired stable, well-paid jobs. Luz is one of them. She started out in house cleaning jobs but now is an experienced counselor at an agency which provides services to Salvadorans. A handful of Salvadorans have progressed from landscape workers to owners of landscaping firms. More frequently, men who began as dishwashers in restaurants have advanced to busboy, assistant cook and even head cook positions. In each of these cases, acquisition of English has been key to advancement. I doubt, however, that first generation Salvadorans will be able to enjoy much more mobility than this because of their limited educations and because returning to school is not a viable option for most given their work and family obligations.

The other major force behind changes in Salvadorans' employment histories is the life cycle, the birth of children in particular. When immigrant women are childless (or their children are in the home country) they tend to maximize earnings by working long hours and often taking back-breaking work. With the arrival of children, they must negotiate among needs. Some desire the stability and benefits (especially health insurance) which are more often available in formal jobs, particularly in unionized factories than in the informal economy. This is the path that Margarita pursued. She cleaned houses shortly after she arrived in the early 1980s. But when she was pregnant with her son, she stopped cleaning and began to search for a factory job which offered health insurance. Though she now works in a factory earning only $6 per hour, she feels satisfied because the job is within walking distance of her home and her son's school. In case of a crisis, she can be home in minutes. Moreover, she compensates for her low income by renting out rooms in her apartment and sometimes cooking for her boarders. The combined strategy provides enough income for her as a single parent to provide adequately for her family but with no frills.

Conclusion

Salvadorans, then, have been drawn to Long Island because of demand for their labor, because wages are slightly higher than elsewhere, and because they have friends and relatives who came earlier. Most have migrated directly to Long Island from El Salvador following these networks of kin and friends. When they arrived they entered the economy at the bottom where many jobs were being created—or vacated— that did not appeal to native Long Islanders. Their status as undocumented immigrants, coupled with their low levels of education and skills—gave them few employment options. Thus, they started at the bottom of the job hierarchy and few have been able to overcome these barriers. Prejudices against Salvadorans' ethnicity and class background (as peasants) appear to have played a part in their destinies as well; this will be discussed in chapter 5.

Regardless of their social status, Salvadorans play an important role on Long Island. At a time when many native Long Islanders are leaving the area owing to its high cost of living, immigrants stay because they, and their families both in the U.S. and in El Salvador, depend on the income from these jobs. Immigrants have learned to offset the high cost of living by living ascetically and tapping multiple sources of income. Finally, the arrival of the Salvadorans has been mutually advantageous. As they earn enough to sustain themselves and their families, immigrants have also buoyed the local economy by being willing to work for low wages in low-status jobs. They have helped to subsidize middle-and upper-class Long Island families' standards of living.

4

Daily Life and Challenges

The sun refracted brightly through the broken window and onto the boys' sleeping faces. Nearby, Yolanda readied breakfast for her sons, Juan, three, and Arnoldo, eleven. Her husband, Edgar, left an hour before. It is late May and homeowners want their pools readied for the Labor Day holiday. Edgar will not return until 9 P.M. after a fourteen hour workday, seven days a week. Yolanda cajoles her sons out of their slumber and through breakfast. Arnoldo will wait for the school bus by himself; Yolanda and Juan must head out early to the first house she will clean that day. While she cleans, Juan must be kept at bay until 10:30 A.M. when she drops him off at a Head Start center for two and one-half hours of structured play with other toddlers. She then returns to the house to finish cleaning and later onto the second house on her schedule. At one o'clock she races back to pick up Juan in her dented ten-year-old station wagon. He will play another hour and then, hopefully, take a nap while she finishes her work. After that they head home to where Arnoldo has been waiting, watching television for an hour. She prepares a quick dinner of rice with vegetables and fried meat. Then Yolanda's mother arrives; she will watch the children while Yolanda cleans yet another house. At nine o'clock Yolanda is back home and Edgar arrives, weary and dusty. His dinner must be warmed and served to him. He then reads Juan a goodnight story and everyone is sleeping by ten or ten-thirty.

The typical day in the Pacheco household leaves little room for socializing. "The people in El Salvador think that the people in the United States are living well in this beautiful country," Yolanda told me. "This country may be beautiful but you don't come here to enjoy the beauty. You come here to work, work, work and the time you have to enjoy it is very minimal." Handling work and domestic duties requires juggling all available resources and the responsibility falls disproportionately on women. Yolanda weaves together shifting work and family schedules into a delicate tapestry that changes from day to day. On Mondays and Wednesdays she performs office assistance for the family where she was employed as an interna, a live-in maid, five years ago. On Tuesdays and Thursday through Saturday she cleans houses, generally two by day and one at night on weekdays. Yolanda's mother and Juan's godmother each take care of the children two evenings per week while Yolanda works. On Monday nights she has been attending GED classes to earn her high school diploma since her Salvadoran diploma is not recognized by the local community colleges. Her goal is to get an associate's degree in secretarial science and return to pink-collar office work, the type of job she last held in El Salvador before fleeing to the U.S.

The Pacheco's life in 1995 is stressful and harried, but they have come quite a distance since 1990 when I first met them. At that time, Yolanda and Edgar were not able to live together. Yolanda was working her job as an interna where she was given a room but no conjugal visits. She was paid only $150 per week for six days of work. Edgar was struggling to find day jobs and rented a room in a make-shift basement apartment. Sunday was the only day they spent together. Yolanda's son, Arnoldo, was living in El Salvador with her brother and being cared for by a neighborhood woman during the day. She worried about him all the time. "My working life has been turned completely upside down," she told me. "In my house in El Salvador I had someone who took care of my son. Here I have come to do the same job but for someone else's child. And I abandoned my own son in the hands of someone else [when I came to the United States]....What you do is come here, abandoning your own children, so that you can try to provide a better future for your children. You don't take care of your own here; you take care of others' children. It's really hard, it costs you a lot and you suffer a lot for this." Yolanda worried not only about her son's safety but also about her brother's security because the military and guerrillas continued to recruit young men like him in San Salvador where he lived. During the summer of 1990, Yolanda financed the immigration of her brother and Arnoldo, then only six years old. For a month she had no news of them and grew exceptionally thin, haggard and anxious. Finally a telephone call came; they were safely in the U.S. but would not be released by their smugglers until Yolanda wired the remaining money. They would not even let her speak to her son. She hurriedly borrowed the remaining sum from her employers—thousands of dollars which would take her more than a year to pay back— and several days later flew to Texas to reunite her family.

Since those dramatic days, the Pacheco's have survived many cycles of boom and bust. They move forward a few steps and then are driven backwards again. The seasonality of Edgar's job is particularly hard. From November through March he is unemployed at the pool company and only occasionally finds other work. Before he applied for TPS (temporary legal status), he had virtually no luck at all except occasional dishwashing jobs. There were just too many other undocumented workers desperate for work during the down months. During the winter, they spend their savings and begin to accumulate debts. Fortunately, Yolanda's work has been steadier except when she became noticeably pregnant with Juan. Yolanda then had to leave her interna job but could not physically withstand house cleaning and other arduous work. That winter she and Edgar were both unemployed for several months and they became indebted. Fortunately, Yolanda's brother held a steady job grooming trees; he sustained the entire household by paying their rent and expenses when the couple's resources were depleted. These funds were later repaid when Yolanda and Edgar began working again.

The Pacheco's cycle is on an upswing in the summer of 1995. Work is plentiful and the household's income exceeds expenses. Yolanda's brother still shares their small apartment, one that has received no maintenance in the years I have visited it and has grown progressively cluttered and shabby. Edgar is busily financing the construction of a house for his extended family in El Salvador, expenditures that siphon off much of his income and consequently have angered Yolanda. The buoyancy from their financial security is deflated by social distance and weariness, the consequences of busy lives. Yolanda and her family are lucky to find half an hour each day when they are together. But they need to take full advantage of the current economic opportunities because they know that at any moment their luck could change, particularly since they will lose their temporary work authorization in 1996.

Immigrants' lives on Long Island move between two poles—work and home, but work constitutes the core of their days and home is the periphery. In the past chapter, I focussed on employment. In this chapter I discuss other aspects of everyday existence, including home life, local institutions, and social time. I also examine issues of social change and cultural differences between life in El Salvador and the United States.

HOUSING AND HOUSEHOLD STRUCTURE

When most Americans think of a household, they envision a family sharing a house or an apartment together. This family may be the classic two-parent nuclear family or it may be a single-parent with children or even an unmarried couple. The key building blocks are closely-related people sharing a common space. Among Salvadorans on Long Island, this type of household is rare. The high expense of housing on Long Island among other factors has created a household structure that contrasts sharply with that of mainstream Americans and also of Salvadorans in their homeland. Nearly all Long Island Salvadorans share residential space with family and non-family; apartments and houses containing six or more adults and several more children are the norm, not the exception. Renting and maintaining an apartment or house requires a minimum of an extended family as in the Pacheco example. This practice of sharing space distributes financial liabilities among several adults in different types of employment, helping to assure that the rent will be paid even during difficult financial times.

In El Salvador, particularly in rural hamlets or caseríos, extended families live next door to each other but not in the same residence. Caseríos are actually constructed around extended families. Jesús' village is a case in point. When I visited him in March 1995, Jesús was building a house of adobe immediately next to his own house. He told me that his eldest son was about to marry and that this new house would become his son's. The other forty or so houses in the caserío all belong to kin related by blood or marriage. Though extended families live in the same vicinity, homes are occupied by nuclear families. Special circumstances may arise which require the combining of several nuclear families or segments of families into one household, but the preferred style is to live separately. While visiting many informants' home towns, I met several migrants who had left their wives and children in El Salvador while they worked most of the year in the United States. These families generally lived with the husbands' relatives (the traditional pattern) while the migrants financed the building of their own homes. The migrants' long-term goal was proximity to, but residential independence from, their relatives.

In El Salvador most people, except the urban poor, own their homes. Migrants from the countryside, who constitute the vast majority of Salvadorans on Long Island, were familiar with paying rent to plant crops on large landowners' properties, but they were unaccustomed to the practice of paying rent for housing. Even when the newly arrived have been forewarned about housing costs in the U.S. by more seasoned migrants, they are shocked and dismayed to have to pay just for a place to sleep. "In El Salvador a peasant has his own house; he's a peasant but he has his own house," Don José began as he tried to explain the differences between life as an agriculturalist in El Salvador and as a worker in suburban U.S. "He has a cow to give him milk. He doesn't use oil, he doesn't pay for fuel because he has firewood...Everyone collects firewood...So, you don't pay for the wood; you don't pay for water because there is a tank and you go and get your water...You don't pay for light, you don't pay any type of taxes. You plant beans, rice, corn and feed for the animals and chiles. You also have your own chickens, pigs, cows; you have your own horses and so you don't have to buy anything...So, those people who are not lazy always have enough to live on. They can always survive even if they don't have a salary...People live, yes they live poorly, logically, because if they have no salary then they will live poorly. But they live. Here they can't live; if a person here doesn't have a salary then how is he going to live?"

A House is not a Home

The rent migrants pay basically buys them a space to rest at the end of a weary day. Sunday afternoons are the periods of greatest social interaction among people who "live" together. The mixture of minimal leisure time and coexistence with nonrelatives and even strangers leaves many Salvadorans feeling that their housing is not a home. "I can't call this home," Don José remarked about the apartment where he lived in Goldcoast. "For me a home is family. You are with your spouse and that is home. But I can't call this home." His commentary is perhaps difficult to understand without a description of his apartment. For more than a year, José shared an two-bedroom unit in a large apartment complex in Goldcoast owned by an absentee landlord from Hempstead. The $1000 rent was split among the shifting population of residents. Three single beds hugged the walls in José's bedroom which he shared with two other men. On one wall workmen had ripped a hole through the sheet rock to repair some leaking pipes and had neglected to patch over the damage. Near José's bed he had hung a mural of a cornucopia overflowing with money, gold and jewels. He told me the mural was an "inspiration" and the subject of much kidding. On top of the cornucopia he had originally written the sum "$2,000,000" but his roommates had added another two, creating a the astronomical figure of $22,000,000. The mural juxtaposed the migrants' kingly hopes, their American dreams, with their spartan reality. A few clothes and a radio were the only other objects in the room.

The apartment's other bedroom was occupied by Amalia, her infant son who was born with a heart ailment, her common-law husband and two other roommates whose beds were separated from Amalia's by a sheet hung on a piece of twine. Next to her bed was a sewing machine; her closet was full of brightly colored material and dresses in different stages of fabrication. In the living room several other men slept on the couch and floor by night. A television glared continuously from the wall by the windows overlooking downtown Goldcoast.

A floor below and around the corridor resided Altagracia, her *compañero* or common-law husband, Edmundo Granados, and their infant son, Edmundo Jr. The small family lived tucked into the bedroom of their one-bedroom apartment. In the living room, four to six men slept boarding-house style. Edmundo had lived for many years as a roommate in someone else's apartment; he finally had saved up the $750 to rent his own but could not afford to live alone with his small family. Shortly after I began to meet with Altagracia and her family, helping them to resolve medical bills from her pregnancy and delivery, Edmundo told me their rent had jumped to $938. I examined his lease and realized that the landlord had slipped a separate sheet into the rent renewal form which was a request form for the parking space. Edmundo and his wife did not own a car; nor could they read English, so they inadvertently signed the parking space authorization only to find their rent increased by $100 for the privilege. Other Salvadorans were similarly targeted and, with help from a local organization, took the landlord to court. The landlord retaliated by seeking Edmundo's eviction on grounds of overcrowding, and won. The family had to move into a room in a friend's apartment. Later they moved to still another apartment occupying one of the three bedrooms and sharing the kitchen and bathroom with some six other adults and four children. Five years later, Edmundo and Altagracia have separated. She and her son sleep on the couch of a tiny apartment while a couple—no relative of Altagracia's—occupy the bedroom.

A final example of immigrant housing on Long Island that depicts the disjuncture between household and family as well as pre- and post-migration housing arrangements is seen in Jesús and Roberto's housing history. Jesús and Roberto met at a sanctuary house—a homeless shelter for undocumented Central Americans run by a local advocacy group—shortly after immigrating from El Salvador. Though they are from different areas of the country, Jesús from Morazán and Roberto from La Libertad, they became friends when they shared adjoining berths in the sanctuary's rough-hewn basement bunkbeds. After a couple of months they moved into the small house rented by Don Federico Chávez from a slumlord in Suffolk County. Roberto slept in a room he shared with another single man and a couple; Jesús slept in the living room with several other men. The "living room" never had a couch; its furniture varied from two to three single beds separated from the entrance by a "world map" shower curtain. The beds were accompanied by makeshift dressers and ringed by several free weights and an aged, black and white television set. Still other tenants occupied the porch and garage out back. A woman with a toddler and infant lived in the second bedroom along with her compañero. Roaches crawled all over the floor and walls in this house, particularly in the kitchen where splatters of grease and food covered the area around the stove. The kitchen floor linoleum was nearly translucent from wear and the stove was covered with grease splatters. The garage doubled as living space for one man and his informal car repair business. Heat in the house was sporadic, the water was occasionally turned off due to non-payment of bills, and the cesspool backed up repeatedly. As in many houses I saw on Long Island, immigrants stored their foodstuffs along with the rest of their belongings in their rooms or labeled the food that they kept in the refrigerator. Friends and relatives often cooked meals together in shifts so that evenings were marked by a succession of food preparations and the stove was never idle. Different groups invited others to try their recipes and occasionally on Sundays large batches of food were cooked and everyone invited to share.

Roberto and Jesús lived for a year or more at Don Federico's before moving into another house in the same town. They set up their cots in the basement and carved out some privacy by hanging up sheets. Upstairs, two couples with children rented the first-floor bedrooms and the second-floor bedrooms were rented to childless couples and a few single men. Over the months that Roberto and Jesús lived in this house its occupants and their location changed continuously. The first summer Roberto and Jesús lived in the basement but later Roberto moved to a bedroom on the second floor that he shared with his nephew. Jesús slept in the living room during the cold winter months and returned to the basement, where the rent was cheaper, the next summer.

These housing arrangements and conditions are typical of those experienced by Salvadorans on Long Island. But this does not mean that Salvadorans *choose* to live this way. Several factors are responsible for their housing patterns. These include (1) the high cost of buying a house and the limited availability of affordable and rental housing; (2) the long legacy of residential segregation by race and ethnicity on Long Island; and (3) immigration patterns and life cycle changes experienced by the immigrants themselves. The first two factors help explain why Salvadorans must share housing with other individuals and why much of this housing is in poor condition. The third factor explains how needs for housing change.

Residential Segregation by Race and Ethnicity

Most of Long Island was built by developers to accommodate middle-class families in their own homes. These homes averaged $202,660 in Nassau County and $163,633 in Suffolk County in 1991 (*New York Times* December 21, 1991). Only 18% of the housing stock is rental units and rents rose dramatically during the 1980s, from a median of $314 per month in Nassau county ($297 in Suffolk) in 1980 to $678 in 1990 ($696 in Suffolk) (*Newsday* May 19, 1991). The result has been a critical shortage of affordable housing, a deficit which led to the creation of an estimated 90,000 illegal apartments (one-third of the entire rental market) carved out of single-family homes by converting basements, attics, and the like into rentable space (*New York Times* April 14, 1991; *Newsday* December 8, 1989). Much of this illegal housing is inhabited by Salvadorans and other immigrants, but there are many native Long Islanders whose low incomes drive them into the illegal housing market as well. Slumlords are responsible for many of the illegal units, but middle-class homeowners seeking to defray high local taxes also participate by converting parts of their homes for rent. This practice is found in many types of neighborhoods all over Long Island, though "minority pockets" have the highest concentrations for reasons I will now explain.

Salvadorans not only tend to live in unusual and often illegal housing, but their residences are often in substandard condition and in areas with clusters of African-American and Puerto Rican populations such as Hempstead, Freeport and Uniondale in Nassau County, and Wyandanch, Huntington Station and Brentwood in Suffolk County. Residential segregation on Long Island is pronounced; according to one study it is the fifteenth most segregated metropolitan area in the United States out of 318 studied (see *Newsday* May 18, 1992). Segregation is most extreme for African-Americans: two-thirds of Long Island neighborhoods are less than one percent black and one-half have no blacks at all. The average white resident of Nassau County lives in a census tract where only 8 percent of their neighbors are black or Latino (*New York Times* March 17, 1994). This is no coincidence; it is the outcome of many decades of practices designed to segregate housing along racial and ethnic lines.

In previous years, the prejudices behind this segregation were more blatant than today. As cited in the introduction to this book, blacks were expressly excluded from Levittown and other mass subdivisions built after World War II by restrictive covenants (*New York Times* June 28, 1992). Abraham Levitt, Levittown's builder, justified this exclusionary policy by suggesting that whites would not buy homes in a mixed neighborhood. "I have come to know that if we sell one house to a Negro family, then 90 to 95 percent of our white customers will not buy into the community," he said (ibid.). Such covenants were common until a Supreme Court ruling made them illegal in 1948 (Jackson 1985:208), but they had already pushed black G.I.s and their families into less restrictive places such as Wyandanch and North Amityville in Suffolk County. Puerto Ricans, drawn to Long Island by labor contracts in agriculture and later in defense manufacturing industries during and after World War II, settled primarily around the Brentwood area.

Segregation of minority populations from the predominant white population on Long Island has also been accomplished by such techniques are redlining, block busting, and racial steering. Discrimination against Latino and Black applicants for mortgages, especially for homes in minority areas, has been a feature of bank lending practices for many years. "Redlining," as outlined earlier, originated in the 1930s when government officials began to color-code maps of neighborhoods according to their desirability and stability: blue for excellent, yellow for passable but often transitional, and red for undesirable. The government backed mortgages only for homes in the blue and yellow areas. Minority neighborhoods were always colored red and thus excluded from FHA assistance (Jackson 1985). Though the color coding is gone, the practice of redlining or evaluating neighborhoods persists. Indeed, it is rising on Long Island while declining in neighboring New York City (*Newsday* August 26, 1993; September 6, 1993).

In "block busting," another practice that produces and perpetuates segregation, agents rent or sell homes to African-American or Latino families and then "scare" white families into believing that the neighborhood is turning over. This tactic yields quick sales and high profits. Blockbusting in the Nassau County town of Uniondale has led to a 25 percent drop in the white population, while the African-American and Latino populations have doubled (*Newsday* September 24, 1990). In 1980, this town was 70% white, 26% black and 7% Latino. By 1990, the white population had dropped to 45% while the black and Latino populations had doubled to 46% and 14% respectively (*Newsday* March 8, 1992).[1] White homeowners were encouraged to sell their homes through alarming letters from realtors. The letters stated that an agent "'will

---

1.   The figures cited are from the 1990 Census. They do not add up to 100% because Latinos are identified separately from race and therefore are counted twice, once by race identification and once by Hispanic origin.

be contacting you from time to time regarding something new happening in our local real estate market'" (*Newsday* September 24, 1990), implying that they should sell their homes before housing prices fell.

Racial steering is the practice by which agents match the race of the renter/buyer to the race of the owner/landlord in order to preserve the racial make-up of a neighborhood. Though banned by New York State law in 1958 and by the Federal Fair Housing Act enacted in 1968, this practice is well-documented on Long Island (see Mahler 1995 for details). One of the most notorious cases to come to light was an apartment referral service in East Meadow. The owner "was accused of having programmed his company's computer to indicate the ethnic background of prospective tenants and landlords, along with the biases of the landlords" (*New York Times* February 15, 1994). He was sued by the state attorney general who cited his actions as exemplary of discriminatory practices by other brokers.

These practices affect Salvadorans' ability to find housing. Margarita, who fled her country to avoid recruitment by the guerrillas as a schoolteacher, claims that brokers and landlords dislike renting to Latinos, particularly those with children. "In the case of housing here in [my town], if you go to a real estate office looking for an apartment, they first ask you which country you are from. They don't ask you for a deposit or for their payment; rather, they ask you 'Where are you from? Are you Salvadoran? Peruvian?' Then they say, 'Oh, no there are many problems with the Hispanics. We don't want to rent to you.' This is how they begin to talk. They don't want to rent to Hispanics....Here [White] Americans are preferred."

Realtors and landlords are not the only culprits involved in persistent residential segregation on Long Island. Neighbors and town leaders frequently protest the arrival of immigrants and other people of color in their towns through such tactics as selective enforcement of local ordinances concerning housing, health and safety codes and those outlawing illegal housing units. The outcome of these various practices is that only a small proportion of Salvadorans live in illegal apartments or rent homes located in white, middle-class neighborhoods. They are located in low-income zones on the margins of middle-class and affluent towns, living in housing owned by Long Islanders who have moved to more expensive areas. Still, by far the largest concentrations of Salvadorans are in well-established "minority pockets." They feel a pervasive sense of separation from mainstream America. By day Salvadorans labor on the grounds and in the edifices of the mainstream population as landscapers and house cleaners, but the houses' owners are away at work. By night, Salvadorans retreat back into their segregated districts. The two groups rarely cross paths except occasionally in the supermarket or post office.

The Encargado System

Faced with the prospect of substandard, often dangerous, and dilapidated housing for high prices, Salvadorans have innovated the *encargado* system, a method for subletting space within housing units (see Mahler 1992, 1995 for more details). The individuals who hold the leases to properties are called the "encargados." They invest several thousand dollars to cover the first month's rent, security deposit, and perhaps the last month's rent. Afterward, they sublet space to enough people so they can turn a profit. At a minimum, encargados wish to cover the rent and utilities expenses so that they, and perhaps their family, can live for free. Don Federico, the encargado with whom Jesús and Roberto lived, claimed to have rented the house for $1200 and charged each tenant around $125 per month. Although the number of tenants vacillated from month to month, the average was around ten. Thus, the rents Federico collected were barely sufficient to pay his fees and also the costs of heat and electricity. But at least one of his subleases told me that he actually paid $800 in rent and was pocketing several hundred dollars each month in profit. Encargados do their best to keep their tenants from knowing the true cost of the unit, fueling suspicions of exploitation. Indeed, I often heard people say that encargados are "doing business with housing." Encargados countered that theirs was a thankless job, that collecting rents was not easy, particularly in the winter months when many people are out of work, and that they must comply with the lease even when their tenants move out suddenly and do not pay.

The encargado system is the outcome of an extremely constricted housing market for Salvadorans and other immigrants. It is not too different from practices dating back at least into the nineteenth century when families would take in boarders or double up with other families in order to economize on housing costs (Mutchler and Krivo 1989). Boarding was a particularly helpful strategy historically among newly-arrived immigrants in the early twentieth century, including Italian immigrants to Long Island (LaGumina 1988). But the encargado system exists during a different time, a time in which many communities have written ordinances restricting the number of unrelated people who may dwell in a housing unit. Out of necessity, immigrants regularly violate these laws although they are generally completely unaware the laws exist. On Long Island these ordinances were not regularly enforced in most communities until large numbers of Salvadorans and other immigrants arrived. Now, rallying around issues of "overcrowding" and "over taxation" of services, many middle-class communities are launching efforts to halt immigration and encourage the newcomers to move elsewhere.

The encargado system lowers the cost of housing for most Salvadorans but it is still too high for some, a largely invisible group—the Long Island homeless. During the summer months in Goldcoast, for instance, a group of Salvadorans occupied an aqueduct tunnel which ran beneath one of the main thoroughfares. On a walkway within the tunnel I found clothing and bedding, even a small bag with men's toilet articles and cologne. As I approached, the men who lived there ran away into the woods where lean-tos had been set up. I recognized some of the clothing and surmised that these were men who frequented the shape-up point nearby but earned too little to afford housing. I confirmed this by interviewing Salvadorans there the next day. This is only one of many hidden sites where immigrants have come to build shelters according to Mark Stamey, a researcher who has studied homelessness on Long Island.

Immigration Patterns and Life Cycles

The forms households take among Salvadorans on Long Island are also influenced by immigration patterns and life cycle changes—particularly marriage (or cohabitation) and the birth of children. The relevant immigration pattern here is whether people came alone or in family groups. In the early phases of my research I found that most Salvadorans were teenagers or men who had left their families at home. They had fled direct persecution or the threat of recruitment by the military or guerrillas. As my research progressed, I began to see more and more women and this pattern has continued. Some women, like Sonia, came following her husband; others were assisted by brothers and other male kin already living in the U.S. Children and elder family members were usually left behind because they would be a financial burden in the U.S. and because the trip was too dangerous for them. "I think that it's hard to have a family here," Jesús explained, "you have to pay rent, pay for food and everything. Maybe with some people who have a place where they can stay, things change. Maybe they have more family members or more possibilities. But for me to bring my family here I'd have to have more money because it costs a lot. If I had the money maybe I'd bring the oldest one up so that he could learn English and other things. But there aren't the resources for this."

Without their families, men such as Roberto, Jesús, and Don José required only minimal housing—a bed and some space to store belongings. This was a convenient arrangement because they had minimal obligations to their encargados and could move frequently to take advantage of job opportunities. As their stays prolong, many Salvadorans finance the immigration of family members or form new families in the United States and this changes their housing needs and costs. When Don José's wife and young son arrived one summer, he tried desperately to rent an affordable room in an apartment for them. His wife felt uncomfortable in José's apartment where they shared a room with Amalia and her family, separated only by a curtain. But his quest was thwarted by the fact that every encargado wanted to charge him rent by the person and not by the room. This he could not afford.

Immigration patterns and housing constraints contribute to the fluidity of household and family structures but there is also another important factor involved: social custom. In the rural areas of El Salvador where most Long Island Salvadorans are from, many, if not most, couples do not marry or marry each other very late in life. The custom is for couples to *acompañarse*, to live together in common-law marriage and perhaps marry in their later years for purposes of inheritance. Children are legitimized vis-a-vis the state through marriage and have less difficulty inheriting the family property than if they are born out of wedlock. Frequently, young men and women will pass through several trial common-law unions, often bearing children in each, before settling into a more long-term relationship. Cohabitation is much less common among the middle- and upper-classes who tend to marry (at least partially to preserve social status) and among those in Protestant evangelical groups. On Long Island I found that the multiple-union pattern, or "serial monogamy" according to anthropologists, is widely practiced except among evangelicals. Noemí Orellana, for example, lived with one man and bore a daughter with him. He returned to El Salvador where it was rumored that he had relationship with another woman. About a year later he came back to Long Island but by this time Noemí had started seeing another man. Her first compañero became enraged but she still left him and later gave birth to another daughter by her second relationship. Sonia and her husband represent another variation on this pattern. They have been married for over fifteen years on paper and have three children, but they have not lived together for the past five years. Her husband has another lover in El Salvador who has born several children by him. Sonia complains bitterly that her husband supports these children but not hers. "*Quieren el gustazo pero no el trancazo,*" she told me referring to men. "They want the fun part but not the responsibility afterward." Many women told me they preferred not to get married because as Catholics they could not get a church divorce and then would be trapped if the marriage soured. On Long Island this practice has more repercussions for women because if their common-law marriage fails, they cannot return back to their parents' household. Few older Salvadorans have emigrated, cutting off women's safety nets. Moreover, Salvadoran women who are single parents find that they cannot afford most childcare; some work at night while their children sleep in the care of relatives or housemates and others send their children back to El Salvador. These decisions are not easy and women agonize them, the strain reflected in their faces.

Household Stress and Its Consequences

Although mutual assistance and cooperation among Salvadorans is common, there is also a lot of suspicion and tension. Salvadorans habitually share food with other members of their households, particularly specialties such as cheese from the homeland. Women babysit each other's children in times of need, friends give each other rides when most people charge for this service, and literate housemates write letters for those who cannot write. Information about jobs, stores with inexpensive prices, and housing alternatives and the like circulate readily among housemates and visitors. Nonetheless, Salvadorans characterize their relations with compatriots in unflattering terms. A typical response to my question concerning co-ethnic relations was, "Salvadorans are not united. They're jealous and competitive with each other." Though I found much evidence to the contrary by observing their daily lives, Salvadorans seemed to overlook the positives and underscore the negatives. Salvadorans feel taken advantage of by their compatriots—angry, for example, when fellow Salvadorans seem to overcharge them for rent and for services such as car rides.

Stress generated within households and brought with immigrants from El Salvador also afflicts Salvadorans. Many Salvadoran parents rely on their children to translate correspondence written in English and to interpret for them during face-to-face encounters with English speakers. This inverts the normal parent-child role and contributes to older Salvadorans' feelings of alienation and loss of power. Simultaneously, husband-wife relations are often strained by the fact that most Salvadoran women work for wages in the U.S. and often find jobs more easily than their spouses or compañeros.

Past experiences affect migrants' stress levels as well. Particularly significant is the trauma from the civil war that has produced psychological distress among the refugees (Farias 1991; Guarnaccia and Farias 1988; Jenkins 1991, 1994). Salvadorans studied by Cervantes and colleagues (1989) were found to suffer from post-traumatic stress disorder (PSTD) to a much higher degree than Mexican immigrants, Mexican-Americans born in the U.S., and Anglo-Americans. Their work suggests that this higher incidence is produced by the legacy of the violence experienced during the war in conjunction with the stresses of migration (e.g., the journey and culture shock).

Salvadorans do not often complain about their economic status in the U.S.; they see their position in relation to their lives in El Salvador. This helps reduce one source of stress in their lives—a perspective generally lost to their children, the second generation. The dilapidated condition of Salvadorans housing is not a topic often complained about, possibly because most grew up with large families in one room houses with no electricity or plumbing; that is, their housing on Long Island is superior to what they left behind. However, there is quite a lot of bickering among housemates regarding general maintenance and conditions of common areas. Among other comments, I heard people claim that others stole food and money or refused to help clean the bathroom and kitchen. This is complicated by people's work schedules.

While landscapers and nannies tend to work during the day, many factory workers are employed at night. There is a constant flow of people into and out of homes; even if rooms are kept locked, there are frequent reports of thefts and disturbances. Additionally, the diverse work schedules keep family and housemates from seeing each other on a regular basis. "[In El Salvador] you don't live very far away from your relatives. Rather, you build your house very close to your relatives," explained Sonia. "Here, no; even if you want to be together you can't. Because there are people who in our

country were from the same town and who lived closely together—even sharing the same patio—but here they don't
have time to visit each other because of their jobs. Days,
months, and years pass by and you can't get together with
other people because of your work." Such conditions make it
very difficult to socialize, to coordinate tasks such as cleaning, and to resolve grievances when they arise.

Suspicion and misgivings toward housemates are also related to people's allegiances during the Salvadoran civil war.
A phenomenon that I call "strange bedfellows" occurs when
Salvadorans who were sympathetic to one side of the civil
war live, owing to the scarcity of housing, in the same place
as Salvadorans sympathetic to the other side. Before the war
ended in 1992, the tension from this predicament would rise
when people started talking about the war. "We tell jokes
about the war," Jesús told me when I asked him how his
roommates, who had different views than his own, talked
about the conflict. "We say sometimes that we have done certain things even though we have not. Those who say they haven't done something probably are the ones who did it. And
those who say they did it are probably the ones who didn't."
The other method commonly employed to diffuse tension
was to assert that everyone had been a victim of the war,
glossing the issue of culpability.

Aside from close quarters and little privacy, years of separation contribute to feelings of jealousy and suspicion experienced by many Salvadorans, especially couples. Carmen's
husband arrived on Long Island a few years before her. When
Carmen came, they shared a room in a house in Brentwood
but she was unhappy there. Carmen told me that she suspected one housemate of having had an affair with her husband.
This is not uncommon. The director of a Long Island wom-
en's health clinic told me that Salvadoran patients who came
in for pregnancy services or treatment of sexually-transmit-
ted diseases assumed that their husbands or compañeros had
been with other women during their separations. A Salvadoran health outreach worker cited a high incidence of domestic
abuse in Salvadoran households. She gave several reasons for
this, including men's alcohol abuse and their anguish that
women find work easier than they do. Gender roles are re-

versed in the U.S. women become principal providers and
men suffer more from unemployment. When these realities
are added to the pressures immigrants are under to provide
for themselves, their families in the U.S. and in El Salvador,
the mixture can become explosive.

Until my return to field research in 1994-5, I had only
heard about domestic abuse from counselors and social
workers but when I reestablished links to informants, several
women confided that they had been victims of physical and
emotional abuse. Among them were Altagracia who separated from her compañero after a severe beating that led housemates to call the police; Yolanda told me of prolonged
emotional abuse and deprivation of financial assistance;
Sonia not only received virtually no financial aid from her
husband, but once was struck by him during pregnancy, almost losing the baby; and Noemí's compañero humiliates her
elder daughter and has also threatened to kill Noemí if she
tries to move away from him. Efforts made by myself and another friend of Noemí's to find her a new home or shelter
have been impeded by the facts that she lacks permanent
legal status and has not been physically abused. These cases
and information from service providers lead me to believe
that domestic abuse is alarmingly widespread. Informants
also have told me that abuse is also prevalent in El Salvador;
thus, it is probably not just a product of migration but a trag-
edy of social marginalization.

COMMUNITY TIES THAT BIND

If structural constraints largely imposed upon Salvadorans
in the wider society pull them apart, other forces bring them
together and foster a sense of community. The life cycle is
marked by rituals that unite people and reproduce their culture at births, baptisms, birthdays, first communions,
quinceañeras (sweet sixteen [actually fifteen] parties) marriag-
es, funerals, and holidays. When money is tight, some of
these occasions pass with little fanfare, but whenever possible they are celebrated with gusto. Eight months into her
pregnancy with Juan, Yolanda was treated to a baby shower.
Friends gave her many pieces of baby equipment and cloth-

ing, knowing that she had to start from scratch. Each guest was given a momento, a ceramic baby carriage with a ribbon engraved with Yolanda's name. Each year thereafter, Yolanda and Edgar have given a birthday party ostensibly for Juan, a celebration also intended as a thank-you to her extended family and friends who have babysat the boy or provided her family with other needed services.

Likewise, when Amalia's son was born and she had to leave her job as a chamber maid in a nearby motel, her friends brought her food and formula for the baby. They advertised Amalia's talent as a dressmaker and helped bring her clients. In return, Amalia occasionally took care of their children in her home or sewed items for them at discount prices. Baptisms and first communions are celebrated at church and serve to knit parents and godparents of the child together as *compadres.* Interviews and observations suggest that these celebrations occur with less frequency on Long Island than in El Salvador. Again, transportation and work schedules preclude some from attending; church services in Spanish are not available everywhere forcing many Salvadorans to travel long distances to attend. The most elaborate celebrations marking life cycle events are weddings among Protestant evangelicals. Usually several couples are married at the same time and the whole congregation is invited—one hundred or more people.

Indeed, the church is one of the principal institutions buttressing the Salvadoran community on Long Island. Actually, there are two major denominations and several other minor ones have many devotees. The major denominations are the Catholic church and the Apóstoles Y Profetas (Apostles and Prophets) church which itself is divided into more and less orthodox branches. Until recent decades, the Catholic church in the U.S. had a tradition of being split into parishes based on national origins. Thus, Goldcoast among other Long Island towns has parishes of Italian, Irish, and Polish heritage. For Puerto Rican and new immigrant Spanish-speaking Catholics, the Catholic church has not created new parishes, but provides mass in Spanish to select churches. Congregants told me that Spanish masses were not always provided voluntarily; many were instituted only after vigorous advocacy campaigns. On most Sundays these masses are filled nearly to capacity; on major holidays such as Christmas and Easter, the celebrants overflow into the walkways within the sanctuary and outside into the foyers.

Members of the Apostles and Prophets church do not suffer from the bureaucratic foot-dragging characteristic of the Catholic church owing to its smaller size and local Salvadoran leadership. This denomination has a large following in El Salvador itself, particularly in northern La Unión department where many Long Island Salvadorans are from. The women evangelicals are readily identifiable by their white lace kerchiefs and by the fact that they never wear slacks. This conservative sect is strict; members are expected to attend long services and refrain from social vices such as alcohol. There are two main congregations of the Apostles and Prophets church on the island, one in Glen Cove and another in Brentwood. These two were united previously until the membership grew too large and they fissioned. Finally, Salvadorans have also joined other Protestant churches such as the Pentacostals, denominations which also have counterparts in El Salvador.

Churches provide not only spiritual guidance but also community support. The Catholic diocese has an extensive outreach program that in many towns offers services such as employment and immigration information and access to its food pantry and used clothing supplies. Catholic and other churches also run soup kitchens that are critical aids to immigrants during bouts of unemployment and other times of need. Their efforts are complemented by other social service agencies such as CARECEN (the Central American Refugee Center) and Centro Salvadoreño in Hempstead and La Unión Hispánica in Central Islip. The Apostles and Prophets church is relatively insular, catering to its own flock. But at least one congregation has forged extensive ties to their community of origin in El Salvador. Thousands of dollars were collected to build a sister church there and to install electricity in the church and to the homes of its membership. The pastor of this congregation returned home for the inauguration of the hometown church, even though he was undocumented and had to return to the U.S. illegally afterwards.

Salvadorans on Long Island have also established many other community organizations that bind them together through organized activities and informal socializing. These include a few Spanish-language newspapers and a cable television and a radio show that broadcasts local information of importance to the as well as information about El Salvador. Soccer is very popular among Salvadoran men, and over the years dozens of teams have been formed and joined into several leagues. Large companies from El Salvador such as TACA airlines and local small businesses help sponsor the teams, but much of their funding is raised through parties and raffles. Adding to social life on the island, especially on weekends, are the abundant Salvadoran restaurants or *pupuserías*—at least a dozen in Hempstead alone. Though there are no Spanish-language cinemas, night clubs have also been established in many towns. A Salvadoran entrepreneur brings music groups from El Salvador and Latin America weekly, providing a home-grown feel to local entertainment

A clear public demonstration of Central American pride and community spirit occurs on one Sunday every September—the day of the Central American Independence Day Parade. Originally organized by a Salvadoran social service agency (CRECEN) and now by an amalgam of local Latino leaders (who dispute over its control), the parade commemorates historical independence and contemporary unity. Bands and colorful floats parade down the streets of Hempstead while onlookers wave their national flags. Beauty princesses and political leaders wave from sports cars and vendors hawk foods.

To my mind, the greatest contributions made toward community solidarity occur informally on Sunday afternoons. Most Salvadorans labor six days a week. On Sunday mornings they do the weekly shopping and the laundry, but by mid-afternoon social time arrives. This is when women are generally found cooking together in the kitchen and when men watch a soccer match or assist each other repairing their cars. During the warm months people congregate at soccer games, around bodegas (small grocery stores), in the parks and at the beach. Visitors arrive and there is a spontaneous barbecue or *sancocho* (meat and vegetable stew) to be shared.

During the big holidays celebrated, Christmas and Easter, women prepare special foods, such as tamales, in mass quantities to be shared with family and friends. The most important aspect of these social hours, whether special occasions or not, is the comraderie and sharing of information that takes place informally. These are moments of relaxation but not of idleness. Social bonds are created and nurtured which are essential to immigrants' lives. With little or no access to government assistance, immigrants derive their social security from their networks. The more dense and extensive these networks, the more people and resources individuals can call on when they are needed.

INSTITUTIONAL MARGINALIZATION: THE U.S. HEALTH CARE SYSTEM

Although much of their lives on Long Island is conducted on the margins of the mainstream, Salvadorans must engage and confront mainstream institutions on a regular basis. Often Salvadorans have a hard time adjusting to the American version of these institutions; institutions also experience difficulty dealing with Salvadorans. The health care delivery system in the U.S., for example, is expensive and operates very differently than in El Salvador. There, medicines are dispensed without prescriptions. Consequently, many immigrants send home for medicines instead of going to a doctor or clinic in the U.S. In any case, few have health insurance through their jobs, and they cannot afford to take time off from work to go to doctors or clinics. Jesús, for instance, suffered an allergic reaction to some shrubbery he was planting during his landscaping job. After several agonizing days with a rash that covered most of his body, he sent to El Salvador for a salve to apply; it arrived some days later with a personal courier. In general, I found that immigrants tried their best to stay healthy; they used home remedies and avoided clinics and hospitals except for emergencies. This pattern changes during pregnancy and following childbirth.

Salvadoran women become more acculturated to the U.S. healthcare system than men because pregnancy and pediatric care draws them into the fold. On many occasions I took women to their prenatal check-ups at local and county-run clinics. Sometimes there were bilingual personnel to serve the Salvadorans' needs, but quite frequently I became an interpreter. The need was often so urgent that once I was identified as bilingual, I would be called in to translate for complete strangers. Moreover, I was also sought to assist pregnant clients fill out the mountainous and complex paperwork to qualify for Medicaid. In New York State, as in other states, undocumented immigrant women who are pregnant may receive Medicaid to cover the cost of births under the rationale that these children will be U.S. citizens. To receive these benefits, they must first prove that they are indigent to and the paper documentation process is daunting. Oscar Zelaya and his wife are from Concepción de Oriente in eastern La Unión Department. They had a baby born with some complications and they applied for Medicaid. Their income level was low enough to qualify, yet because Oscar's wife was listed as a beneficiary of her brother's bank certificate of deposit in case of his death, their application was denied. Paperwork is not the only barrier to access. Sonia filed for Medicaid for her two children who were born in the U.S. Both came down with severe cases of the flu in the winter of 1995 and she had to take them to a local clinic. On the $5,000 per year she makes cooking hamburgers at McDonalds, she could not afford to pay the clinic bill nor for the medicines prescribed. But their Medicaid case was denied when Sonia could not find a ride to the her interview at the Department of Social Services.

TRANSNATIONAL OBLIGATIONS

Although Salvadorans' lives on Long Island revolve around a core of work and a periphery of home and social life, they also involve ties between the U.S. and El Salvador. "The processes by which immigrants build social fields that link together their country of origin and their country of settlement" are referred to by contemporary scholars of migration as "transnationalism" (Glick Schiller, Basch and Szanton Blanc 1992:1). Salvadorans do not enjoy permanent legal status so they cannot return to El Salvador for a visit any time they want. They have had to devise ways to maintain links to their homeland without going home themselves. They communicate by phone, through letters sent by courier agencies, and through individuals, like Don Apolinario Lemus, who have legal status and travel back and forth providing various personal services for a fee. Once a month, Don Lemus, known to Salvadorans as "Poli," receives letters, money, and packages from his clients (mostly extended relatives from his hometown of Polorós in La Unión Department), flies to El Salvador, and then delivers the goods personally. When he returns to the U.S., he carries a reverse flow of letters, medicines, legal documents and cheese. Poli provides an important service to his clients in both countries; he transmits important information as well. Salvadorans also maintain linkages homeward through hometown associations. These are formed by groups of immigrants from the same area in El Salvador who raise funds to finance improvements in their home towns. The editor of one of the local Long Island Spanish-language newspapers belongs to an organization that aids his home town, Chiquirín, also in La Unión. I have been told that there are several other associations in existence on Long Island (*Tribuna Hispana* July 5, 1995); many more have been formed in Los Angeles and other areas of the U.S.

Transnationalism helps fill a longing most Salvadorans have for their homeland. The older they were when they migrated, the stronger this feeling is. Edmundo told me that there is a saying which expresses this yearning for home: *"donde deja el umbligo, nunca se olvida"* ["You never forget the place where you were born"]. These ties are more than nostalgic, however. Immigrants bear the burden of supporting family in El Salvador and also financing new homes or repairs to their old homes there. In order to save money for these investments from their paltry salaries and informal economic activities, Salvadorans make sacrifices. Sometimes they deprive themselves of comforts; sometimes they refuse assistance to people who ask for help. The strain can be overwhelming, as Sister Maria learned. "When I was in the hospital, and [my daughter] was going to be born I had nothing for her," she recalled. "My cousin had bought her a few things, but I had nothing else because I didn't have any money. And my mother in El Salvador wanted me to send her money because I was in the United States. And they didn't know that I wasn't working. She wanted to know why I didn't send her money. She thought that I had come here to work and to help them. They didn't know that I couldn't work. So what I did was take the little money that my cousin gave me for the baby send it to my mother. But when I had my baby I didn't have a crib, nothing, not even diapers or blankets to wrap her in. I had to tell this to the nurses in the hospital and they didn't want to give my baby to me because I didn't even have clothes to dress her in."

CULTURAL CHANGE AMONG SALVADORANS

No matter how much Salvadorans on Long Island look back to their past, they cannot recover it. They have changed. The overt signs of acculturation to American ways are everywhere Salvadoran families frequent McDonalds for an inexpensive family meal out; young men like Jorge Ayala, who only a few years ago worked the fields of their forefathers in heavy boots and cowboy hats, now sport punk haircuts and wear neon-colored spandex bike shorts with tie-dyed tee-shirts. Even Salvadorans who migrated as full-fledged adults have changed dramatically—like Santos, a man I met shortly after he arrived in the U.S. At that time, he still exuded the air of the quintessential transplanted peasant. Green to the core, Santos looked spellbound at the skyscrapers in Manhattan when he went to his first political asylum hearing. Unfamiliar with how to eat a sandwich given him for lunch, he carefully peeled off each layer of the first half and consumed tomato, lettuce and cheese separately. Within a year of his arrival, Santos had forsaken his work boots for shiny black cowboy boots and a stylish denim jacket with a rock band insignia embroidered on the back. And he proudly drew a Citibank electronic teller card from his velcro wallet, although he confided that he had no idea how to use it. Though still a landless peasant in El Salvador, Santos had penetrated Long Island chic.

It is essential not to confuse such examples of cultural assimilation with more fundamental integration into the core institutions of the new society labeled "structural assimilation" (Gordon 1964). Salvadoran immigrants remain very marginalized. However, they feel that they have experienced significant changes in the United States. Among those most frequently mentioned are changes in the pace of life and intensity of work and the transformations of gender roles.

Time seems to fly by in the United States whereas it crept slowly in El Salvador, particularly in the countryside where there was ample time to socialize. Life in the U.S. seems to be sped up like a movie in fast forward. One dashes to work, to the baby sitter, to the store, to school, and to home. And there is little people can do to slow the pace down. Time has become money and money is always in short supply. "[In El Salvador] you're not obligated to work," Gilberto Canales remarked. He grew up as a peasant and fled El Salvador after he was tortured by a death squad. His brother and father were murdered later. "You work out of *cariño* [love]. Sometimes you work hard but you work with more cariño because it's your own land. Yes, I mean you work with more *voluntad* [willingness]. Because you work for yourself, you are happy with the work you're going to do. But here, no." When I asked Gilberto why he worked here, he responded, "Because if you don't work you won't have a place to stay, even though you don't live comfortably anyway. Sometimes you don't even earn enough to pay the rent."

For Gilberto, work has become an obligation he cannot shirk. For several years he labored for a construction firm where his salary increased from $65 to $125 per day. When the company folded, he could find no job that paid as well, despite having his green card. Gilberto now sweats through 12-hour days in the laundry of a large seafood restaurant making only $3.80 an hour. His sister and mother in El Salvador depend on his remittances, regardless of the fact that his income has plummeted.

Gilberto is not married but when I asked him, hypothetically, if he would want his wife to work in the U.S. he answered, "If I had a wife then she'd have to work here like me. If she had money in her pocket then she's the owner. And the same is true for me." Gilberto is articulating an attitude toward women's roles that reflect change. "In El Salvador only the husband works," explained Margarita. "There the man is in charge and the wife has to do what her husband says. Even today this is the custom. Here no. Here I work, I earn money and I help him pay the expenses as much as I can but I do with my money what I want. I administer my money, not [my husband]. We help each other share the expenses. But I administer my own money. It's different in El Salvador because there the husband gives the wife money. And if the husband says it's okay to buy a dress then [the wife] buys it but if it is too expensive then he won't let her. Here women are different, they're more liberal."

This newfound independence is a source of stress on relationships. Men often like to feel they are in control even when their spouses work. They come home and expect to be served meals and women generally oblige, but feel torn. They enjoy earning money but know that their status as good women is primarily a function of being faithful wives and mothers. This ambivalence resonates in the voice of Sonia: "Women, particularly from the countryside, change. They come here and work and they earn dollars. They see a weekly paycheck. They get full of themselves, some of them become *malcriadas* [bad tempered] and begin to speak very crudely. Now they aren't submissive any more. They tell their husbands, 'Go away! Go away. I don't love you anymore.' ....Before they never worked and never had money in their power. But here they do and it's their money that makes them more independent."

Whereas some changes immigrants experience may be empowering to migrants, others are disempowering. Relations with bureaucracies, in particular, are often humiliating and frustrating, leaving immigrants feeling marginalized. Noemí learned this under tragic circumstances. From birth, her second child, Sara, was sickly. She was always running a fever and her development was stunted. Repeated visits to the doctor and two hospitalizations did not reveal the source of her affliction. Noemí could not work outside the home because Sara required constant attention. Then one day I received a call from Noemí. Sara was in the hospital and very ill. Two days later, not even a month past her first birthday, she died. Despite her shock, Noemí was expected to negotiate the unknown cultural terrain of death and dying in the U.S. She and the baby's father agreed to an autopsy only to find out that it would not be performed until Monday, two days later. In El Salvador, the family holds a *velorio*, a wake, in their home the night of the death and the father arranges for burial, including digging the grave himself. Noemí and her compañero were required, in complete contrast to their custom, to leave Sara's bedside a few hours after the baby died. To their great anguish they could not hold a wake or grieve communally until several days later when the body was released. Every effort that I and other friends made to get the child home sooner was thwarted by bureaucracy and the weekend. As the funeral director explained, "In America, don't die on the weekend." Though Sara's death underscored immigrants' alienation from American institutions and practices, it promoted Salvadorans' solidarity. Friends dropped by, donating hundreds of dollars for the burial and for a headstone, and the funeral was well-attended. Each weekend Noemí visits the site placing fresh flowers amidst the cross, ceramic toys and balloons decorating the grave. Months after the death, however, she still had not received the results of the autopsy despite repeated efforts.

Each day and each month Salvadorans face obstacles and challenges. Though they pass from greenhorns to seasoned migrants, the trials never cease. Successes are always threatened by setbacks, but this does not mean that there are no achievements, no milestones along the way. Most Salvadorans I have known do progress over time. Like Edgar and Yolanda, most have enjoyed some degree of socioeconomic mobility over the past five years and this is truly an accomplishment. Yet despite two incomes they have moved up the ladder barely a rung, from the near-homeless to the working poor. And this position is tentative. In 1995, nearly 200,000 Salvadorans covered under temporary protected status (TPS/DED) lost this status and in 1996 they will lose their work authorization. This worries Salvadorans everywhere. They are also keenly aware that the political climate in the United States is turning against them. For years they were denied status as refugees and the benefits that come with that status; now they fear mass deportation. And the suburbs that so conveniently embraced their labor do not want them as neighbors and do not want to finance their children's education.

5

Acceptance or Resistance? Long Islanders Meet the Newcomers

On September 12, 1989 throngs of people headed toward the Goldcoast Town Hall as the sun began to set on what had been a balmy, late summer day. Never before had the building accommodated so many people; there was no room to sit and the crowd spilled out into the foyer and onto the steps. What drew them to attend was nothing less than the future of their community, a community which had become an ethnic and class crucible. The crowd was clearly divided into two camps: the established suburbanites and the newcomer immigrants. In the front of the hall well-groomed Long Islanders were seated, sporting designer suits and khaki trousers with docksiders. Behind them, seated and standing, stood legions of Salvadoran men in soiled jeans and work boots whose rough-hewn hands bespoke their occupations as landscape laborers and construction workers. Visible from any angle was the glaring reality that suburbanites cannot isolate themselves from issues of immigration and poverty, issues long been associated only with big cities.

The meeting was held to address grievances against a meeting place for day laborers—a shape-up—which many townsfolk wished to eliminate. On the table was a proposed ordinance aimed at prohibiting people from congregating for the purpose of seeking a job. The shape-up itself embodied the radical demographic changes Goldcoast was undergoing. It was located in front of "Lucia's Deli," a locale stocked full of Italian staples which catered to the descendants of Italian immigrants who had come to Goldcoast in two waves, first at the turn of the twentieth century and later after World War II. Conveniently situated in the heart of the old Italian settlement area, the deli preserved local traditions—except for two notable peculiarities. First, dozens of Salvadoran day laborers congregated there in the early mornings during the good weather months; and second, the deli's owners were newly arrived immigrants from Korea, not Italy.

The town hall meeting was the second phase in a strategy promoted by the mayor of Goldcoast, the son of Italian immigrants, to rid the town of the shape-up. Some days before, a request he made to the Immigration and Naturalization Service (INS) had been granted. The INS raided the shape-up and twenty-six people were arrested, almost all of them undocumented immigrants from El Salvador. These immigrants were placed in deportation proceedings, but the raid had a more profound impact. The number of job seekers at the deli dropped to a handful the next day and remained low for weeks. The raid frightened immigrants and angered their advocates, while many local residents were happy to see some attention paid to what they viewed as an eyesore, a symbol of a town perched precariously close to social decline and blight.

The town hall meeting offered the next opportunity for conflict. Defendants of the status quo squared off against the protagonists of social change. The mayor promoted the ordinance to the audience as a measure aimed at preserving Goldcoast's quality of life: "'We will not allow our city to become the center for illegal aliens congregating and taking away what people here have worked so hard for,'" he argued. Established residents echoed this theme in their remarks. "They're urinating on the building. We've caught them in the backyard [of my father's house]. They leave litter,'" testified one man, the descendent of Italian immigrants. Another man claimed that his car had been broken into three times near the deli, insinuating but offering no proof that the day laborers were the culprits (*Newsday* September 13, 1989). And a prominent Puerto Rican, allied with the mayor, pointed to a young girl and alleged that the day laborers made cat calls and harassed women patrons and even girls like her. Advocates for the Salvadorans rose to defend them, explaining how they had fled their country to save their lives and how they worked hard to support themselves and their families.

None of the Salvadorans present actually spoke because the hearing was conducted in English and few understood the debate. The hearing served to underscore these immigrants' marginalization from Goldcoast and mainstream American life as a whole. Only later was I able to gain insight into their perspective on the deli through formal interviews. In general, Salvadorans asserted that while some people who congregated at the shape-up might commit "uncultured" acts such as urinating in public, the majority were law abiding residents, people merely seeking a day's hard labor. Don José lived in the town for a year or two prior to the INS raid and ordinance issue. At first he felt no discrimination but later he realized that there was a lot of hostility being directed at the Salvadorans and other Latinos in town. "When I originally came here there wasn't this rejection but now, yes. The police hassle Hispanics everywhere. As soon as they see the face of a Hispanic inside a car they immediately turn on their lights and stop his car to ask him for his papers." When I asked him what he thought would improve the situation, he responded, "We have to form a workers' union because that way we would have power. We should create a trade union or a club where everyone can get together and where the bosses can come to get workers." For several months after the September town hall meeting, this idea of a union was actively pursued by immigrants and their advocates but it was never realized.

Yolanda told me that "It would be nice if the mayor would recognize that what he is doing is not right...[Immigrants] are not prejudicing the community; rather, they are helping the community because their labor makes [Long Islanders'] houses shine. If there weren't people out there ready to work, the community wouldn't have its houses in such fine shape and the community wouldn't look so good. It's the illegals, the Hispanics who are doing the work." Yolanda's comments point to the symbiosis between newcomers and established residents, a theme that I have stressed in this book. No one at the meeting ever acknowledged this relationship; the meeting, the INS raid and letters to the local papers asserted that immigrants do not make a positive contribution to the community. The proposed ordinance even implied that immigrants entice Long Islanders to perform illegal activities—the hiring of undocumented workers. Salvadoran immigrants were depicted as evil doers while their employers were exonerated and portrayed as victims, even though the employers and the residents benefited most from the immigrants' cheap labor.

ANTI-IMMIGRANT SENTIMENT: WIDESPREAD AND GROWING

In recent years, there has been a consistent anti-immigrant backlash all over the Long Island. The ordinance and immigration raid against day laborers in Goldcoast is but one of many efforts mounted to discourage immigrants, Salvadorans in particular, from settling in many communities on Long Island. Other examples include the tightening of housing ordinances in Freeport, Manorhaven, Oyster Bay and other towns. Bayville even hired a private detective to search for illegal apartments (*Newsday* September 17, 1993). Many communities have instituted strict admissions policies for their schools, requiring tenants to obtain affidavits from their landlords stating who legally resides in their units in order to register children for school. In Elmont, the campaign to ferret out registrants who are not true residents of the school district was carried to an extreme. The principal of an Elmont elementary school sent the names of the families of two undocumented immigrant children to the local congressional representative who forwarded the information to the INS, even though these children have a constitutional right to an education. Fearing deportation, the families fled the town and the school—illegally—saved itself the cost of the children's education. In Montauk, residents complained to East Hampton Town officials about "huge crowds, blasting radios and spectators urinating in bushes during Hispanic soccer games at Lions Field. (*Newsday* September 17, 1993).

Another illustration of anti-immigrant feeling on Long Island was the 1993 repeal of a Suffolk County ordinance that had protected Central Americans by barring public officials from reporting them to the INS. Moreover, in 1994 the Suffolk County legislature overwhelmingly approved a resolution asking New York State for permission to deny health care and welfare benefits to legal as well as undocumented immigrants. The title of the resolution was the "America First Welfare Reduction Program" and even though the state refused the county's request, the effort sent a strong message that immigrants are not welcome on Long Island.

The 1993 the mayoral election in Goldcoast provided another arena for Long Islanders to blame immigrants for their community's ills. Both the Republican and Democratic party candidates, themselves descendants of Italian immigrants, promised to work aggressively to address the "illegal alien situation." The Republican candidate advocated that the city seek out "illegal persons" to keep their children from attending schools because the school district had been "inundated with illegal residents and their presence has ultimately overburdened the system'" (*Record Pilot* October 7, 1993)). He also led a raid on an immigrant home that allegedly violated housing ordinances through overcrowding; the event made the cover of a local newspaper. His Democratic challenger, who would go on to win the election, stressed in his campaign how city services were being taxed by the newcomers.

> "People are coming here for a better way of life. We have to sympathize with them, but [Goldcoast] is saturated. The schools are filled up, emergency rooms are filled, and as many as 20 unrelated people are living in some houses. Play by the rules," he said, "and we'll help you" (ibid.).

After taking office in 1994, the new mayor began a widespread crusade against overcrowding and illegal housing units, efforts that disproportionately affected Salvadorans. He also negotiated the relocation of the town's shape-up to an area out of public view. When I interviewed him in June 1995, he readily admitted that his efforts are designed to discourage more immigrants from settling in Goldcoast.

Anti-Immigrant Wave Extends Beyond Long Island

The backlash against immigrants and the push to restrict their influx and to assimilate those already in the U.S. has, by no means, been limited to Long Island or the New York metropolitan area. Quite to the contrary, the most significant endeavors, such as the English Only movement and Proposition 187, were launched from other states. A national English Only movement was introduced by Senator S.I. Hayakawa of Hawaii in 1981, but it was based on a landmark ordinance passed by voters in Dade County, Florida (Miami) in November of 1980. This ordinance reversed a county-wide policy of official bilingualism and biculturalism dating back to 1973 (Castro 1992). The Miami antibilingualism movement signified "a vehicle for the expression of mass native white resistance to Latinization and was a political project aimed at symbolically reestablishing Anglo dominance" (ibid.:122).

Just as the Miami campaign spurred similar efforts elsewhere in the country, California's Proposition 187 in 1994 sparked numerous copycat initiatives in other states. Proposition 187, known as the "Save Our State" (SOS) initiative, was principally aimed at denying undocumented immigrants access to public services such as healthcare, education and cash assistance. It also contained a provision which would require service providers to report suspected "illegal aliens" to California's Attorney General and to the INS. Under Proposition 187, school teachers, nurses and hospital personnel would effectively become INS agents. The proposition was approved by California voters by a margin of 59 to 41 percent; 64 percent of whites, 57 percent of Asian Americans, 56 percent of African-Americans, and 31 percent of Latinos voted in favor of it (Martin 1995). Shortly after approval, the law was questioned on constitutional grounds and a federal judged barred its enforcement. But the symbolic victory was still sweet: a forceful message had been sent to Washington and south of the border that the people of California want immigration curbed. California—much like Goldcoast—let it be known that it no longer welcomed newcomers, at least those of a certain hue. And the Proposition 187 banner was adopted by people in several other states including Florida and New York.

Anti-immigrant sentiment is also not unique to the United States. Actually, in recent decades the U.S. has been a much more hospitable place for foreigners than most other immigrant-receiving countries. Germany, for instance, does not grant citizenship to the children of immigrants who are born on its soil whereas anyone born in the U.S. is entitled to citizenship. Both Germany and Japan readily permit people whose heritage is ethnically German or Japanese (such as Peruvians and Brazilians whose parents or grandparents emigrated from Japan) to immigrate back to the "homeland" but severely restrict immigration of other national groups. Neo-Nazi movements in Germany have also targeted immigrants, sometimes attacking them on the streets or firebombing their homes. In France, one of the contenders for the presidency in the 1995 elections was Jacques Le Pen. He gained political favor through years of blaming immigrants for that country's economic problems. Skinheads (white supremacists) attending one of his rallies pushed a Moroccan immigrant into the Seine river in Paris and he drowned. Mosques have been defaced with anti-Islamic graffiti. And in 1994, France adopted a policy of disallowing girls to wear veils at school, claiming that this Arab custom was divisive and violated that country's tradition of secular education (*New York Times* September 11, 1994; May 6, 1995). In sum, a climate of restrictionism and intolerance of foreigners has become pervasive in many, if not most, immigrant-receiving countries. This has occurred at a time when more and more refugees and migrants have become uprooted from their homelands and are hoping to relocate in safer places and countries offering the possibility of greater opportunities. They are finding the golden door closing, if not shut entirely.

CAUSES OF ANTI-IMMIGRANT SENTIMENT AGAINST SALVADORANS ON LONG ISLAND

The causes of anti-immigrant sentiment or nativism are complex and vary from setting to setting. Anti-immigrant sentiment is on the rise in the U.S., I would argue, for two main reasons: (1) economic insecurity—produced by broad structural changes in the national and global economies and (2) the fact that immigrants are no longer confined principally to the inner cities but are increasingly entering the heartland—suburbia.

The events in Goldcoast offer a way to begin to understand the complex dynamics behind this rise in nativism. Long Island's economy was so strong during the 1970s and 1980s that it actually drew labor from neighboring New York City as well as from overseas. At the end of the 1980s, however, cuts in defense spending and the downsizing and restructuring of many manufacturing and service corporations threw Long Island into its first fiscal crisis. Unemployment rates rose, taxes were hiked to cover deficits in municipal spending despite large budget cuts, and many families defaulted on their mortgages. Residents tightened their belts and local governments cut expenditures and programs throughout Long Island. Mayors and budget managers looked for places to pare spending and services to immigrants, most of whom are not citizens and therefore cannot vote. They became an optimal target. The current mayor of Goldcoast is no exception. He told me that, while he sympathized with the Salvadorans' misfortunes during the civil war, the town could not solve all the problems of the world. His job was to be attentive to the concerns of his constituents, such as a 70 year-old widow on a fixed income trying to pay her real estate taxes who complains that they rise each year in order to pay for services to the newcomers. Established residents, fearful that the newcomers were destabilizing their neighborhoods as well as driving up their taxes, were pressuring him to "get these people out of here."

Economic restructuring affects virtually every layer of American society: companies create scores of minimum-wage jobs, hire more part-time and temporary workers, scale back or eliminate benefits, and require permanent employees to work longer hours to compensate for positions that have been eliminated (E.g., Sassen 1988). Immigrants have become scapegoats for these economic problems. On Long Island there was virtually no backlash against immigrants until the economic recession of the late 1980s and early 1990s. The incidents mentioned above all occurred in 1989 and afterward, coinciding perfectly with the downturn in the economy. This is not surprising given that, historically, nativism has typically arisen during times of economic and/or political turmoil (see Higham 1963 for a thorough discussion).

In places like Goldcoast, another key factor in the wave of anti-immigrant sentiment is the threat immigrants represent to suburban middle-class security. In mainstream, white, middle-class American culture, the bedrock of future security is real estate—the investment in a home. Immigrants to communities on Long Island have not threatened the jobs of the established residents, but they do appear (at least to residents) to threaten real estate values. For white homeowners who, on average, have made a $250,000 investment in their house, the influx of immigrants is alarming. Whites associate the arrival of minorities with the imminent decline in the quality of their neighborhoods and hence, in the value of their properties (Farley et al. 1994). Even during times of relative security and unthreatened employment, they will abandon neighborhoods as soon as a few minorities begin moving in (Massey and Denton 1993) seeking to get out before the property values fall too drastically.

On Long Island, residential segregation kept minority residents restricted to a few towns and neighborhoods until the 1980s. The early Salvadoran immigrants found housing in these same places and felt little resistance to their arrival. As their numbers swelled and they were accompanied by immigrants from other countries in Latin America, they began to settle outside prescribed areas and also gathered visibility on the streets of middle-class towns.

In Goldcoast, Salvadorans are highly visible for two principal reasons: they walk and they appear dark-skinned and poor. Given their low earnings, many Salvadorans cannot afford cars; they walk or bicycle to work, to school and to social events. They also have a distinctive appearance: the majority have jet-black hair, deep-brown skin and sport gold-fillings and bridgework in their teeth. Moreover, men are attired in work boots and jeans and they return home dusty and sweaty from their landscaping and construction jobs. On Sundays and holidays they gather to socialize in front of the local bodega and restaurants. Since most Salvadorans live in crowded apartments, the street is one place where they can get together in groups. Group fraternizing is also a characteristic of social patterns in El Salvador. However, middle-class residents feel intimidated by the presence of men, "hanging out" on the street. These concerns were voiced by Goldcoast residents during the hearings on the shape-up ordinance and they were expressed to the mayor when he visited the town's neighborhoods. People also picked up the phone to report immigrants who kept strange hours—coming and going at all hours of the night, did not mow their lawns, and failed to keep their garbage discretely out of sight.

During his interview, the current mayor of Goldcoast agreed with me that the Salvadorans' visibility was key, that they constitute only several hundred people in a town of 25,000, but leave a disproportionately strong image in established residents' minds. Their concern was that these groups of Salvadoran men, loitering on the street, created the impression of a town in decline, and this, in turn, would affect real estate values. The mayor concluded that that the bottom line was racism. "People don't want to live with people with brown skin." What he did not mention specifically is that Goldcoast's established residents feel financially insecure, and believe that demographic changes rather than economic restructuring lie at the root of the problem.

This helps to explain the anti-immigrant fervor Long Islanders and Americans in general feel, even though cheap immigrant labor helps reduce their expenses. Politicians are clever to confound race with class and economic issues. They play to voters' fears and misperceptions by claiming that immigrants displace American workers, even though most academic and government studies consistently reject this claim (e.g., Borjas 1990; U.S. GAO 1988; Bean et al. 1987; Simon 1989). The controversy in Goldcoast illustrates this confusion and it is not an isolated case. Micro-level ethnography of this area serves to illustrate the consequences of much more macro-level forces on people living in towns throughout the country.

WILL NEWCOMER VS. ESTABLISHED RESIDENT CLASHES CONTINUE?

Are ethnic and class crucibles like Goldcoast a passing phenomenon or is the antagonism toward immigrants likely to continue into the future? I believe that these conflicts will continue into the twenty-first century as more suburban towns experience an influx of newcomers. Each community will have to determine whether the newcomers will be welcomed or resisted. What kind of immigrant-established resident relations develop in each suburb depends on who the newcomers (and established residents) are, how quickly they come, how many there are, and what image they present.

Of course, issues of contact and clash predate the current time period. Indeed, the roots of sociology and urban anthropology are implanted in the study of immigrant-native relations. Generations of anthropologists and sociologists who have studied these relations argue that they have been marked by varying degrees of resistance, even outright violence (see DeSena [1990] for a fine discussion; Rieder 1985; Lamphere, Stepick and Grenier 1994; Takash-Cruz 1990). Two prominent early sociologists, Ernest Burgess and Robert Park, developed models of contact and assimilation with unidirectional stages. Park's model (1924;1925) suggested that different groups would come into contact, compete and clash, then accommodate each other. Ultimately, the children of immigrants would assimilate into the dominant culture. Burgess' theory of concentric zones (1925) postulated less assimilation and more displacement. New arrivals—immigrants—to a city would first hit immigrant areas like a "tidal wave" pushing older immigrants into the next zone of working class residences, who then pushed the better-off families into the next zone. Ultimately, the impact would reach the suburbs. According to Burgess, this process of population distribution preserved "individuals and groups by residence and occupation" (1925:54).

Although one model leads to assimilation and the other to what sociologist Herbert Gans terms "urban villages" or what now might be termed an "ethnic enclaves," the two models essentially posit a limited period of upheaval followed by stasis. Will this happen to the Salvadorans on Long Island? Elderly Italians I interviewed in Goldcoast could recall how they were taunted and deemed inferior when they arrived as immigrants into that town. Decades later, second and third generation descendants of these immigrants predominate in government and local businesses. Perhaps in fifty years the mayor of Goldcoast will be of Salvadoran descent. However, I am not overly optimistic that this will come to pass.

Salvadorans on Long Island will have a difficult time assimilating to the mainstream, I feel. This is because they have two major strikes against them: their physical appearance and their class background. Immigrants from other Latin American countries such as Peru, Colombia and Chile, have fared better on Long Island than the Salvadorans despite the fact that most also came as undocumented immigrants. These immigrants tend to have lighter skin than the Salvadorans, but, more importantly, they are almost exclusively from the middle classes in their countries. Many were professionals in their homelands; they have more education and skills than the Salvadorans and have progressed more over the years that I have studied them alongside the Salvadorans. Indeed, the South Americans in Goldcoast expressly refused to support the Salvadorans during the hearings on the shape-up. Many have tried to distance themselves as much as possible from the Salvadorans, expressing anger that established residents have blamed all Hispanics—and do not distinguish Hispanics by national group or class—for Goldcoast's ills. Don José was chagrined to discover that his good relations with other Latinos was based on their assumption that, due to his polished Spanish and well-groomed appearance, they assumed he was South American not Central American. In sum, among Latino groups on Long Island, Salvadorans may be the most numerous but they are also widely seen as pariahs.

SALVADORANS' PROSPECTS FOR THE FUTURE

Aside from their position in the pecking order, there are more important reasons to be skeptical that Salvadorans will follow the same pathway as past generations of immigrants. Some critics argue that contemporary (post-1965) immigrant groups are unwilling to assimilate into mainstream American culture, that they wish to preserve their differences as "unmeltable ethnics" (Glazer & Moynihan 1970; Schlesinger 1992). Others contend that residential segregation by race affects assimilation. Theorists of "segmented assimilation" argue that assimilation forces still continue to operate but that the children of immigrants will assimilate to the dominant group in their area. That is, children living in mostly white neighborhoods will assimilate to the mainstream while children living in mostly African-American or Latino areas will assimilate into those subcultures—and thereby not experience as much socioeconomic mobility (Portes & Zhou 1994). It is too early to tell which path Salvadorans will take. Salvadoran teenagers in the Long Island town of Hempstead, for example, go to a high school where there are no whites and where the majority of the students are African-American. Students and educators there have told me that the two groups do not mix, but this may change in the next decade as large numbers of Salvadoran children who are in elementary school today move into high school.

In my view, the future for Salvadorans and other recent immigrant groups is not terribly bright for other reasons. A key concern is their low educational achievement. Salvadorans have among the lowest levels of formal education of all immigrant groups. Although several researchers have shown that immigrant children tend to outperform native-born students of their own national/ethnic group, parents' education is a good predictor of children's educational achievement (e.g., Ogbu 1990, Suarez-Orozco 1989, Gibson 1988). Salvadorans also tend to be residentially concentrated in poor neighborhoods with deficient school systems, like Hempstead and Wyandanch. This means that it is harder for them to acquire the education and skills needed to get ahead in society. In Los Angeles, some second-generation Salvadorans have spurned education altogether and become incorporated into violent youth gangs; hundreds of these youth have been deported to El Salvador where they have formed gangs and terrorize entire communities. Fortunately, Salvadoran gangs have not reached Long Island, but they exist in nearby New York City.

Another major obstacle to Salvadorans' future prospects is the economy and the opportunity structure they face. Over the half-dozen years I have been studying Salvadorans on Long Island I have observed most of them go from penniless, jobless recent arrivals living in overcrowded and substandard housing to solid members of the working-class. Though they have made significant gains they have only risen to the level of the working poor, still living in crowded and substandard housing. I do not feel that most will progress much further in their lifetimes unless they obtain more education and skills. Many Salvadoran adults do go to school for English classes and other training, but the fact that most work more than one job, take odd shifts, or cannot afford childcare, makes it difficult for them to further their education. The outlook for Salvadorans' children is not much better. In past years, it was the children and grandchildren of turn-of-the-century immigrants who, buoyed by the post-World War II expanding economy, unionization, and opportunities through the G.I. Bill, among other factors, were propelled en masse into the country's middle-class. The children of Salvadorans and other contemporary immigrants are unlikely to get these bootstraps to pick themselves up with. They face a different economy, one that creates few well-paid manufacturing and other blue-collar jobs and one that has seen the number and power of unions fall dramatically.

Trends in Salvadoran Migration

Despite this bleak prognosis, Salvadorans keep leaving their country, even though the civil war in El Salvador ended in 1992. Continued emigration is fueled largely by the fact that young adults are frustrated by limited educational and job opportunities. Students in the countryside are staying in school longer than their parents (who usually went to school for a only year or two and then started helping with farm chores). Remittances from family members in the U.S. help support this effort. Higher levels of education among young Salvadorans have had important consequences for the rural areas where most Long Island Salvadorans are from. The younger generation does not want to become farmers; they feel they are too educated for this work. They are not educated enough, however, to get good jobs in the cities. Unable to afford continuing their education in distant cities where the only high schools are located, many young people decide that their best option is to go to the United States. Some even told me they hoped to earn enough money to continue their education in El Salvador later. In the meantime, with only nine years of education, they can only hope to get poorly paid jobs in the U.S.

Salvadoran youth are also emigrating because their parents want them to leave. Indeed, new migration patterns are developing. During the civil war youth fled because they feared being recruited into the military or guerrillas. Now they are asked to leave when a parent returns home. For example, Jesús returned to El Salvador in 1993 because his wife needed help raising their family and planting the land. He is currently arranging to finance his second son's trip to the U.S.; the family needs money to buy fertilizers, clothing and school supplies, and to pay for medical expenses. When Jes_s lived in the U.S., his remittances covered these costs while his family raised their own food; when he returned, this source of income disappeared. Many Salvadoran families find themselves in similar circumstances. They have become dependent upon remittances. Sometimes the head of the family spends part of the year in the U.S. and the rest in El Salvador (this is called circular migration), and sometimes older children migrate so that the pattern becomes inter-generational.

The evolution of Salvadoran migration toward circular and inter-generational patterns indicates that it is becoming evermore transnational. People maintain strong ties to their homeland and culture, often travelling back and forth between their native and adoptive countries (Glick Schiller et al. 1992; Basch et al. 1994; Rouse 1992). On the one hand this can be a positive phenomenon, assisting people in retaining their identity and making contributions to their home societies. On the other hand, such transnationalism, as well as many Salvadorans' stated desire to retire back in El Salvador, keeps migrants' primary focus glued to their homeland. This "return mentality" can be detrimental to the groups' progress if it depresses investment in improving their lives, and therefore also their children's lives, in the U.S.

Despite their longing to return, relatively few Salvadorans go back home permanently and, even when they lose their temporary legal status, they are not likely to leave the U.S. in large numbers. Salvadorans attribute this reticence to high levels of crime in El Salvador and few job opportunities. Even those who go back to El Salvador with the intention of staying permanently, often return to the U.S. some months later claiming they could no longer adapt to life back home. "There are poor folk who spend many years here in [the United States] and they don't accomplish anything," Sonia began. "Well, if you are here three years or maybe four and you're working and not wasting your money then you generally can go home with money in your pocket. But if you stay over three or more then maybe you won't take any money back...You begin to forget about your country; you forget about your past poverty and if you are able to return, you end up coming right back to this country and you're happy to make it your home again. You start living with someone, start having children and you're here to stay." She herself returned to El Salvador for three years but spent the entire time determined to return to the U.S. There simply was no future for her and her children there.

Though Salvadoran immigrants and their children are in difficult straits, there is no way to predict their future on Long Island and in the U.S. in general. Perhaps fifty years from now there may even be a shrine on the U.S.-Mexico border to the hundreds of thousands of Salvadorans who crossed it, escaping civil war at home. Probably no immigrants passing through the halls of Ellis Island at the turn of the twentieth century would have dreamed that this crowded, filthy way-station would someday become a shrine and that their names would be immortalized on a plaque overlooking New York Harbor. But this did come to pass and there are some hopeful signs in the new generation. Salvadorans on Long Island and in other parts of the U.S. are graduating with law and medical degrees and many more hopefuls are filling the ranks of elementary schools. They are proud that they and their parents who, against tremendous odds, survived a brutal civil war, a perilous journey to safety, years of feeling tongue-tied because they couldn't speak English, exploitative employers and landlords, and numerous other travails. Theirs has been an epic of survival and they bring this fortitude into the future.

References

Americas Watch
1987 The Civilian Toll 1986-1987: Ninth Supplement to the Report on Human Rights in El Salvador. New York: Americas Watch.

Anderson, Thomas P.
1971 Matanza: El Salvador's Communist Revolt of 1932. Lincoln, NB: University of Nebraska Press.

Armstrong, Robert and Janet Shenk
1982 El Salvador: The Face of Revolution. Boston: South End Press.

Baldassare, Mark
1986 Trouble in Paradise: The Suburban Transformation in America. New York: Columbia University Press.

Barry, Tom
1987 Roots of Rebellion: Land and Hunger in Central America. Boston: South End Press.

Basch, Linda, Nina Glick Schiller and Cristina Szanton Blanc
1994 Nations Unbound:Transnational Projects, Postcolonial Predicaments and Deterritorialized Nation-States. Amsterdam: Gordon and Breach Publishers.

Baumgartner, M.P.
1988 The Moral Order of a Suburb. New York: Oxford University Press.

Bean, Frank D, Edward E. Telles and B. Lindsay Lowell
1987 Undocumented Migration to the United States: Perceptions and Evidence. Population and Development Review 13(4): 671-690.

Berger, Bennett M.
1972 [1961] "The Myth of Suburbia." In John Kramer, Ed. North American Suburbs: Politics, Diversity, and Change. Berkeley, CA: The Glendessary Press.

Birmingham, Stephen
1978 The Golden Dream: Suburbia in the Seventies. New York: Harper & Row, Publishers.

Borjas, George
1990 Friends or Strangers: The Impact of Immigrants on the U.S. Economy. New York: Basic Books.

Bluestone, Barry and Bennett Harrison
1982 The Deindustrialization of America: Plant Closings, Community Abandonment, and the Dismantling of Basic Industry. New York: Basic Books.

Bulmer-Thomas, Victor
1987 The Political Economy of Central America Since 1920. Cambridge: Cambridge University Press.

Burgess, Ernest W.
1925 "The Growth of the City. An Introduction to a Research Project" In Robert E. Park, Ernest Burgess and Roderick D. McKenzie, The City. Chicago: University of Chicago Press.

Calavita, Kitty
1981 "United States Immigration Law and the Control of American Labor." Contemporary Crises 5:341-68.

Carmean, Rachel L., Frank P. Romo, and Michael Schwartz
Not Dated. "Proposal for Research: Plant Locational Decision Making On Long Island." Institute for Social Analysis, SUNY at Stony Brook.

Castells, Manuel and Alejandro Portes
1989 "World Underneath: The Origins, Dynamics, and Effects of the Informal Economy." In Alejandro Portes, Manuel Castells, and Lauren A. Benton, Eds. The Informal Economy: Studies in Advanced and Less Developed Countries. Baltimore, MD: The Johns Hopkins University Press.

Castro, Max J.
1992 "The Politics of Language in Miami." In Guillermo J. Grenier and Alex Stepick III, Eds. Miami Now! Immigration, Ethnicity, and Social Change. Gainesville, FL: University Press of Florida.

Cervantes, R.C., Salgade de Snyder, V.N., Padilla, A.M.
1989 Posttraumatic Stress in Immigrants from Central America and Mexico. Hospital and Community Psychiatry 40: 615-169.

Cornelius, Wayne A.
1982 "Interviewing Undocumented Immigrants: Methodological Reflections Based on Fieldwork in Mexico and the U.S." International Migration Review 16(2):378-411.

Deere, Carmen and Martin Driskin
1984 Rural Poverty in El Salvador:Dimensions, Trends, and Causes. Geneva: International Labour Office, World Employment Programme Research.

DeSena, Judith N.
1990 Protecting One's Turf: Social Strategies for Maintaining Urban Neighborhoods. New York: University Press of America.

Dunkerley, James
1988 Power in the Isthmus: A Political History of Modern Central America. London: VERSO.

Durham, William H.
1979 Scarcity and Survival in Central America: Ecological Origins of the Soccer War. Stanford, CA: Stanford University Press.

Farias, P.J.
1991 Emotional Distress and its Socio-Political Correlates in Salvadoran Refugees: Analysis of a Clinical Sample. Culture, Medicine and Psychiatry 15: 167-192.

Farley, Reynolds, Charlotte Steeh, Maria Krysan, Tara Jackson and Keith Reeves.
1994 "Stereotypes and Segregation: Neighborhoods in the Detroit Area." American Journal of Sociology 100 (3):750-780.

Fishman, Robert
1987 Bourgeois Utopias: The Rise and Fall of Suburbia. New York: Basic Books, Inc.

Fong, Timothy P.
1994 The New Suburban Chinatown The Remaking of Monterey Park, California. Philadelphia, PA: Temple University Press.

Funkhouser, Edward
1991 "Emigration, Remittances, and Labor Market Adjustment: A Comparison of El Salvador and Nicaragua." Paper presented to the 15th Congress of the Latin American Studies Association, April 3, 1991. Washington, DC.

Gans, Herbert
1967 The Levittowners: Ways of Life and Politics in a New Suburban Community. New York: Vintage Books.

Gibson, Margaret A.
1988 Accomodation without Assimilation: Sikh Immigrants in an American High School. Ithaca, New York: Cornell University Press.

Glazer, Nathan and Daniel P. Moynihan
1970 Beyond the Melting Pot: The Negroes, Puerto Ricans, Jews, Italians, & Irish of New York. Cambridge: MIT Press.

Glick Schiller, Nina, Linda Basch, and Cristina Szanton Blanc
1992 "Transnationalism: A New Analytic Framework for Understanding Migration." In Towards a Transnational Perspective on Migration: Race, Class, Ethnicity and Nationalism Reconsidered. Nina Glick Schiller, Linda Basch and Cristina Szanton Blanc, eds. Pp. 1-24. New York: New York Academy of Sciences.

Gordon, Milton M.
1964 Assimilation in American Life: The Role of Race, Religion, and National Origins. New York: Oxford University Press.

Grier, Eunice S. and George Grier
  1988   "Minorities in Suburbia: A Mid-1980s Update." Project No. 3730-01 Prepared for the Urban Institute Symposium on Residential Mobility and Minority Incomes, April 21-22, 1988. Washington, D.C.: Urban Institute.

Guarnaccia, P.U. and Farias, P.
  1988   The social meanings of nervios: A case study of a Central American woman. Social Science and Medicine 26: 1223-1231.

Hamilton, Nora and Norma Stoltz Chinchilla
  1991   "Central American Migration: A Framework for Analysis." Latin American Research Review 26(1): 75-110.

Hannerz, Ulf.
  1980   Exploring the City: Inquiries Toward an Urban Anthropology. New York: Columbia University Press.

Hawkins, John
  1984   Inverse Images: The Meaning of Culture, Ethnicity, and Family in Postcolonial Guatemala. Albuquerque, NM: University of New Mexico Press.

Jackson, Kenneth T.
  1985   Crabgrass Frontier: The Suburbanization of the United States. New York: Oxford University Press.

Jenkins, J.H.
  1994   Bodily transactions of the passions: el calor among Salvadoran women refugees. In Csordas, T., Ed., Embodiment and experience: The existential ground of the self. Cambridge: Cambridge University Press.

———.
  1991   The state construction of affect: Political ethos and mental health among Salvadoran refugees. Culture, Medicine and Psychiatry 15: 139-165.

Kasarda, John D.
  1995   "Industrial Restructuring and the Changing Location of Jobs." In Reynolds Farley, Ed. State of the Union: America in the 1990s. New York: Russell Sage Foundation.

Kramer, John, Ed.
  1972   North American Suburbs: Politics, Diversity, and Change. Berkeley, CA: The Glendessary Press. Higham, John
  1963   Strangers in the Land: Patterns of American Nativism 1860-1925. New York: Atheneum.

LaFeber, Walter
  1983   Inevitable Revolutions: The United States in Central America. New York: W.W. Norton & Company.

LaGumina, Salvatore J. Ed.
  1980   Ethnicity in Suburbia: The Long Island Experience. New York: Salvatore J. LaGumina.

_____.
1988   From Steerage to Suburb: Long Island Italians. Staten Island,
       NY: Center for Migration Studies.

Lamphere, Louise, Alex Stepick, and Guillermo Grenier, Eds.
1994   Newcomers in the Workplace: Immigrants and the Restructur-
       ing of the U.S. Economy. Philadelphia: Temple University
       Press.

Loescher, Gil and John A. Scanlan
1986   Calculated Kindness: Refugees and America's Half-Open Door,
       1945 to the Present. New York: Free Press.

Long Island Almanac
1989   Long Island, NY: Long Island Business News.

Mahler, Sarah J.
1995   American Dreaming:Immigrant Life on the Margins. Princton,
       NJ: Princeton University Press.

_____.
1993   "Alternative Enumeration of Undocumented Salvadorans on
       Long Island." Final Report for Joint Statistical Agreement 89-46,
       U.S. Bureau of the Census.

_____.
1992   "Tres Veces Mojado: Undocumented Central and South Ameri
       can Migration to Suburban Long Island." Ph.D.diss., Columbia
       University.

Martin, Philip
1995   "Proposition 187 in California." International Migration Review
       29(1):255-263.

Massey, Douglas S. and Nancy A. Denton
1993   American Aparthied: Segregation and the Making of the Un-
       derclass. Cambridge, MA: Harvard University Press.

Millman, Joel
1989   "El Salvador's Army, A Force Unto Itself." New York Times
       Magazine. Sunday, December 10, 1989.

Montes, Segundo
1986   El Agro Salvadoreño (1973-1980). San Salvador, El Salvador:
       Editores, Universidad Centroamericana José Simeón Cañas.

Montes Mozo, Segundo and Juan Jose Garcia Vasquez
1988   Salvadoran Migration to the United States: An Exploratory
       Study. Hemispheric Migration Project, Center for Immigration
       Policy and Refugee Assistance, Georgetown University.

Mutchler, Jan E. and Lauren J. Krivo
1989   "Availability and Affordability: Household Adaptation to a
       Housing Squeeze." Social Forces 68(1): 241-261.

Newsday

September 13, 1989. "Ban on Job Seekers Stirs Debate."

November 22, 1989. "From Haiti to Suffolk. Journey's End. The Life and Death of Seven Immigrants."

December 8, 1989. "Planners Say Long Island Needs Its Illegal Aparments and Must Declare Amnesty."

September 24, 1990. "A World Apart. Segregation on Long Island."

May 19, 1991. "Long Island: Still the Family Suburb."

March 8, 1992. "State: Racial Steering Persists; LI Home Brokers Deny Charge."

May 18, 1992. "Pattern of Bias; Study: Segregation marks LI Housing."

February 10, 1993. "Problems of Child Care All Too Familiar on LI."

September 6, 1993. "Red, White and Black; It's Shameful. LI Lenders are Redlining: Denying Mortgages to People of Color."

August 26, 1993. "Home Loan Hurdles for Blacks."

September 17, 1993. "Melting-Pot Rage: On LI, Simmering Anger over Undocumented Hispanics."

April 4, 1995. "The Flight to the Suburbs."

New York Daily News

November 10, 1989. "Call 'em Vans of the Oppressed."

New York State Business Statistics Quarterly Summary.

1989 Albany: New York State Department of Economic Development, Division of Policy Research, Bureau of Business Research.

New York State Department of Labor (NYS DOL). Annual Labor Area Report: Nassau-Suffolk SMSA.

Fiscal Years 1988, 1990. New York: New York State Department of Labor, Division of Research and Statistics, Bureau of Labor Market Information.

New York Times

April 14, 1991. "'Underground Helps Find Low-Cost Housing.'"

December 21, 1991. "After Decades of Growth, Long Island Confronts Stagnation."

June 28, 1992. "At Forty-Five, Levittown's Legacy is Unclear."

February 15, 1994. "L.I. Apartment Service Accused of Bias in Rental Offers."

March 17, 1994. "Persistent Racial Segregation Mars Suburbs' Green Dream."

May 15, 1994. "The Latinization of Allentown, Pa", New York Times Magazine

September 11, 1994. "France Bans Muslim Scarf in its Schools."

Oboler, Suzanne

1995 Ethnic Labels, Latino Lives: Identity and the Politics of (Re)Presentation in the United States. Minneapolis: University of Minnesota Press.

O'Connor, Mary I.
1989 Women's Networks and the Social Needs of Mexican Immigrants. University of California: Social Process Research Institute.

Ogbu, John U.
1990 "Minority Status and Literacy in Comparative Perspective."
Daedalus 119:141-168.

Park, Robert E.
1924 "Social Contacts and Race Conflict." In Robert E. Park, Ernest W.
Burgess, Eds., Introduction to the Science of Sociology. Chicago: University of Chicago Press. Park, Robert E., Ernest W. Burgess and Roderick D. McKenzie
1925 The City. Chicago: University of Chicago Press.

Pearce, Jenny
1986 Promised Land: Peasant Rebellion in Chalatenango El Salvador. London: Latin American Bureau. Portes, Alejandro and
Robert L. Bach.
1985 Latin Journey: Cuban and Mexican Immigrants in the United
States. Berkeley: University of California Press.

Portes, Alejandro and Min Zhou
1994 "Should Immigrants Assimilate?" The Public Interest Summer

Record Pilot
September 14, 1989. "Glen Cove's Move to Bar Undocumented Aliens
from City Streets Brings Storm of Protests."
March 1, 1990. "Ordinance to Ban Solicitation of Employment on
Streets Draws Large Crowd at City Council Meeting."
October 7, 1993. "Mayoral Candidates Meet in Debates." Reynolds,
Malvina.
1963 Little Boxes and Other Handmade Songs. New York: Oak Publi-
cations.

Rivera-Batiz, Francisco L. and Carlos Santiago
1994 Puerto Ricans in the United States: A Changing Reality. Washington, D.C.: The National Puerto Rican Coalition, Inc.

Rieder, Jonathan
1985 Canarsie: The Jews and Italians of Brooklyn against Liberalism.
Cambridge, MA: Harvard University Press.

Rouse, Roger
1992 Making Sense of Settlement: Class Transformation, Cultural
Struggle, and Transnationalism among Mexican Migrants in
the United States. In Towards a Transnational Perspective on
Migration: Race, Class, Ethnicity and Nationalism Reconsidered. Nina Glick Schiller, Linda Basch and Cristina Szanton
Blanc, eds. Pp. 25-52. New York: New York Academy of Sciences.

Sassen, Saskia
1988   The Mobility of Labor and Capital. Cambridge: Cambridge University Press.

Scandlyn, Jean Naomi
1993   "When the Social Contract Fails: Intergenerational Interethnic Conflict in an American Suburban School District." Ph.D. Dissertation, Columbia University. UMI dissertation Services.

Schirmer, Jennifer
1993   "The Seeking of Truth and the Gendering of Consciousness: The CoMadres of El Salvador and the CONAVIGUA Widows of Guatemala." In Sarah A. Radcliffe and Sallie Westwood, Eds. 'Viva' Women and Popular Protest in Latin America. New York: Routledge.

Schlesinger, Arthur M., Jr.
1992   The Disuniting of America. New York: W.W. Norton & Company.

Silk, James
1986   Despite a Generous Spirit: Denying Asylum in the United States. Washington, D.C.: U.S. Committee for Refugees and American Council for Nationalities Service. Simon, Julian L.
1989   The Economic Consequences of Immigration. Oxford: Basil Blackwell and the Cato Institute.

Smits, Edward J.
1974   Nassau: Suburbia, U.S.A.. Garden City, New York: Doubleday & Company, Inc.

Stanback, Jr., Thomas M.
1991   The New Suburbanization: Challenge to the Central City. Boulder, CO: Westview Press.

Su·rez-Orozco, Marcelo M.
1989   Central American Refugees and U.S. High Schools: A Psychological Study of Motivation and Achievement. Stanford, CA: Stanford University Press.

Takash-Cruz, Paule
1990   A Crisis of Democracy: Community Responses to the Latinization of a California Town Dependent on Immigrant Labor. PhD Diss., University of California, Berkeley.

Thruelson, Richard
1976   The Grumman Story. New York: Praeger.

Tribuna Hispana, La.
July 5, 1995. Salvadoreños de New York Trabajando por su Tierra Natal.

(U.S. Committee for Refugees)
1991   USCR Running the Gauntlet: The Central American Journey
        Through Mexico. Washington, DC: American Council for Na-
        tionalities Service. U.S. Department of Commerce
1993   "Persons of Hispanic Origin in the United States." 1990 CP3-3.
        Washington: GPO. U.S. GAO. (U.S. General Accounting Office)
1988   Illegal Aliens: Influence of Illegal Workers on Wages and
        Working Conditions of Legal Workers. Washington, DC: GPO
        (PEMD-88-13BR).

Wattenberg, Ben J. and Richard M. Scammon
1972   "The Suburban Boom." In John Kramer, Ed., North American
        Suburbs: Politics, Diversity, and Change. Berkeley, CA: The
        Glendessary Press.

Whyte, William H.
1956   The Organization Man. New York: Simon and Schuster.

Wolf, Eric
1959   Sons of the Shaking Earth: The People of Mexico and Guatema-
        la, Their Land, History and Culture. Chicago: University of Chi-
        cago Press.

Woodward Jr., Ralph Lee
1985   Central America: A Nation Divided. 2nd Edition ed. New York:
        Oxford University Press.

Yago, Glenn, Wu, Sen-Yuan, and Seifert, Charlene S.
1987   "Long Island: Coming of Age in the 21st Century." Long Island
        2000: Report on Economic Development. Economic Research
        Bureau, Harriman School for Management and Policy, SUNY at
        Stony Brook.

Zhou, Min
1992   Chinatown: The Socioeconomic Potential of an Urban Enclave.
        Philadelphia, PA: Temple University Press.

Zolberg, Aristide R, Astri Suhrke, and Sergio Aguayo
1986   International Factors in the Formation of Refugee Movements.
        International Migration Review; 20(2): 151-169.